DEDICATION

To my family, who loves me even when I'm annoying; my friends, who are always up for an adventure; and those who support my creative and ambitious goals.

Bay Shore County Park

100
THINGS TO DO IN
GREEN BAY
BEFORE YOU
DIE

Packers Heritage Trail

100 THINGS TO DO IN GREEN BAY BEFORE YOU DIE

SARAH CONERY

REEDY PRESS

Reedy Press
PO Box 5131
St. Louis, MO 63139, USA
reedypress.com

Library of Congress Control Number: 2024939002

ISBN: 9781681065366

Design by Jill Halpin

Front cover image and all interior images are courtesy of the author.
Back cover author headshot photograph by Mary Breuer.

Printed in the United States of America
24 25 26 27 28   5 4 3 2 1

CONTENTS

Sports and Recreation

Culture and History

Shopping and Fashion

ACKNOWLEDGMENTS

There are so many people I'd like to thank for helping me along this journey. If I were to list them all individually, I would need about 20 pages to share all of the ways people have supported me during this process. I'd like to thank all of the friends, I've made while living in Green Bay who helped me explore and make this city my home, including but certainly not limited to Olesya, Gabe, Alison, Amanda, Megan, Anastasia, and Tori. My best friend, Katie, who continuously called to check in on how I was throughout the process, kept me going until the very end.

The strong women entrepreneurs I've gotten to know at the Nest Cowork + Club in Green Bay have given me a sense of belonging within the community, and their support makes me feel unstoppable. I am forever thankful for them. Shout-out to Tina, Lauren, Lea, Amanda, and Chelle for their kindness and encouragement while I wrote this book.

Thank you to the friends I've met through the Midwest Travel Network, who have encouraged me and offered support when no one in my immediate circles quite understood the intricacies of my creative pursuits. Specifically, I'd like to thank Nicole for being my accountability partner of sorts.

I'd like to thank my family for giving me space when I needed it and being tolerant of my continuous shenanigans. Finally, I'd like to thank the Reedy Press team, who provided me resources and were patient with me throughout this process as a first-time author.

PREFACE

After living in Green Bay for over nine years, I still feel like I am discovering new favorite spots and learning more fascinating things about the city and the people who call it home. It has been such a pleasure to learn the stories of local entrepreneurs and community members while conducting research for this book.

While there are easily 100 more things I could have featured in this book, I had to stick to a limit of 100 things to highlight. It was incredibly hard to choose which activities to highlight because there are so many great things to do in our area. When it came to choosing, I focused on historic sites, small businesses that have been operating in the area an extended period of time, and companies that were founded in Green Bay.

Green Bay has been voted "Best Place to Live in the US" by *U.S. News & World Report* due to affordability, health care, community resources, and the job market, which are all great things that Green Bay absolutely has covered. What the research doesn't show are the kind people who make Green Bay so welcoming. They are the people volunteering at community events, making it their personal mission to welcome newcomers, and starting conversations with you at the grocery store. These little actions by people in the community are what make Green Bay special. It may just be the "Midwest nice" our region is so famous for, but I like to think there's a special something to our city that keeps people coming back.

I hope that this book helps to guide you in your adventures around Green Bay. When you're exploring and discovering new things, I hope you get to see how beautiful and diverse our community is. Additionally, I hope you enjoy your time in Green Bay so much that you want to come back and visit us again. Happy exploring!

St. Brendan's Inn Pub

FOOD AND DRINK

1

SIP COFFEE
AT KAVARNA

The word *kavarna* means café or coffeehouse in Czech, and Kavarna has been serving coffee-loving locals in Green Bay since 1999. You'll find this café in a distinct yellow Egyptian Revival–style building in the Broadway District. Kavarna is a community hub for local artists, showcasing guest pieces on the walls. It offers ample space to work and free, speedy Wi-Fi for visitors. While most associate Kavarna with good coffee, they are also known for their vegetarian and vegan food.

Sustainability is a priority for Kavarna's owners, Kayla and Mike, who work with local producers and co-ops to bring fresh-quality foods to their café. They roast coffee beans with an eco-friendly electric drum roaster and send food waste to be composted locally. Their commitment to sustainability doesn't stop there; a portion of every coffee sale at Kavarna goes directly to coffee farmers to help improve their farms and communities.

143 N Broadway, 920-430-3200
kavarna.com

MORE PLACES TO GRAB COFFEE

Coffee Wizardz
536 Greene Ave., Allouez
coffeewizardz.com

Daily Buzz Espresso Bar
124 E Walnut St., 920-940-0130
dailybuzzgb.com

Glas Coffeehouse
228 N Adams St., 920-272-2222
glascoffee.com

The Frappe Spot
1910 University Ave., De Pere, 920-819-2421
thefrappespot.com

Luna Café
2665 Monroe Rd., De Pere, 920-632-7626
lunacafe.com

Bhava Coffee
1538 W Mason St., 920-544-0003
bhavacoffee.com

The Attic
730 Bodart St., 920-435-6515
theatticcorner.com

The Exchange Coffee, Mercantile & Eatery
317 Main Ave., De Pere
theexchangecoffee.com

Grounded Café
300 S Adams St., 920-448-4303
groundedcafegb.org

EAT A PANCAKE THE SIZE OF YOUR FACE

AT THE PANCAKE PLACE

The Pancake Place is a 40-year-old family diner known in the area for the massive plate-sized pancakes they serve. With more than 13 fillings to choose from, you can custom order a flavorful pancake to start your day. Another fan-favorite dish is the heaping plate of stuffed hash browns. The Pancake Place prides itself on being a family-friendly restaurant that serves great food at affordable prices with best-in-class service.

The restaurant has been nominated for and awarded over 25 community-choice Best of the Bay Awards in categories of best breakfast, best brunch, best overall restaurant, and best family establishment. Along with local awards, the restaurant has received an award from Tripadvisor.

143 Military Ave., 920-499-2221
eatpancakeplace.com

TIP

The Pancake Place is open daily from 5 a.m. to 2 p.m., so plan accordingly if you're thinking about grabbing a late lunch. Also, if you haven't had an Oreo pancake, this is the place to get one!

BITE INTO A FRESH BAGEL

FROM LOX, STOCK 'N BAGEL CAFE

If you're searching for the freshest bagels in the area, look no further than Lox, Stock 'N Bagel. Whether you prefer plain bagels, bagels with cream cheese, or bagel sandwiches, you won't be disappointed. The bagels here are baked fresh daily, and they're known for their breakfast bagel sandwich. On any given day you will find more than 20 bagel flavors to choose from.

If you think nothing pairs better with fresh bagels than fresh blended cream cheese flavors, you'll enjoy choosing from 10 different cream cheese spreads mixed daily. While at Lox, Stock 'N Bagel, you'll also find a full coffee bar serving Collectivo Coffee, a variety of bakery options, and free Wi-Fi in the dining space.

1300 S Webster Ave., Ste. 103, 920-432-9244
loxstocknbagel.com

TIP

Try the sun-dried tomato basil bagel and make it a breakfast sandwich!

DEVOUR CHEESE CURDS
WITH HOMEMADE RANCH

Eating deliciously salty, gooey fried cheese curds is essential to any itinerary for Green Bay. But the question is, where should you get these cheese curds? You can find fried cheese curds on the majority of restaurant menus in Green Bay, but make sure that, wherever you order them from, there is a side of homemade ranch to accompany them. I dare say that cheese curds and ranch go together better than eggs and bacon.

It's not hard to find fantastic cheese curds in Green Bay, but finding the best homemade ranch to go with cheese curds has become a fun little game for me. If you want to search for the best cheese curd and ranch combo in Green Bay I'll give you a head start. Begin your search at Anduzzi's Sports Club with a basket of their hand-battered, fried Wisconsin white cheddar cheese curds.

1992 Holmgren Way, 920-965-1111
anduzzis.com

OTHER PLACES TO ORDER FRIED CHEESE CURDS

Dykesville Bowl
6426 Sturgeon Bay Rd., Luxemburg, 920-866-9846

Crown & Common
1139 Main St., 920-930-1250
crownandcommon.com

The Bar - Holmgren Way
2001 Holmgren Way, 920-499-9989
meetatthebar.com

Kroll's East
1658 Main St., 920-468-4422
krollseast.com

Kroll's West
1990 S Ridge Rd., Ashwaubenon, 920-497-1111
krollswest.com

Mackinaw's Grill & Spirits
2925 Voyager Dr., 920-406-8000
mackinaws.com

Fox Harbor Pub & Grill
348 S Washington St., 920-593-8327
foxharborpubandgrill.com

SAMPLE THE BEST KRINGLE IN NORTH AMERICA

FROM UNCLE MIKE'S

Uncle Mike's was opened by a third-generation baker in 2001 with a location in De Pere. Just three years later they had to expand because they were running out of space. They now have four locations and have won more than 100 awards for their baking and cake decorating. One of their accolades includes being awarded the title of "Best Kringle in North America" for their sea-salt caramel pecan kringle.

A kringle is a Danish pastry made with 36 layers of buttery, flaky dough shaped like a big pretzel with a filling. Kringles are very popular in Green Bay, thanks to Uncle Mike's, and are the favorite dish of any work potluck, baby shower, or brunch. Uncle Mike's has nine regular kringle flavors and 13 seasonal ones that are available during select times of the year. When visiting the bakery, you'll find kringles and so much more!

1840 Dickinson Rd., De Pere, 920-330-0300
unclemikesbakeshoppe.com

STOP BY
THE BOOYAH SHED

Booyah is a northeast Wisconsin specialty that can be found in the region at community events from tailgates to fairs and festivals. Booyah is a thick stew with chicken, pork, or beef and a variety of veggies and seasonings that sometimes takes days to cook to perfection. When completed, the dish typically serves hundreds of people. In addition to being found at community events, you can find booyah on menus around Green Bay.

If you're on the hunt for booyah, the Booyah Shed is a classic Green Bay restaurant that is sure to give you a taste of this delicious specialty. It started in the area as a food truck before moving to their current permanent location. They offer a variety of homemade foods for customers with the option to dine in or take out. In addition to booyah, menu items include chili, burgers, wraps, sandwiches, poutine, and desserts.

1800 S Ashland Ave., Ste. 3702, 920-371-6249

TIP

Another menu item to try is the beer brat burger! It's a brat without the casing formed into a burger patty. It's my new favorite way to eat brats. Oh, and don't forget to get a slice of Door County cherry pie for dessert.

GO INTO
A PHOCOMA

PhoComa is a family-owned restaurant serving pan-Asian dishes, which include Hmong, Thai, Laotian, and Vietnamese foods. Popular PhoComa menu items are pho, pad thai, orange chicken, egg rolls, bubble tea, and fresh-squeezed lemonade. The Lor family began selling prepared foods and drinks at a farmers market before opening the restaurant in 2019.

PhoComa has a bright welcoming atmosphere and serves up some of the best orange chicken I've ever had. You can try PhoComa dishes while dining in or by placing a takeout order. A hearty meal at PhoComa is sure to bring a smile to your face and then a desire to take a nap after you're full of warm, delicious food.

154 N Broadway, 920-401-8012
phocoma.com

HAVE LUNCH
AT NOT BY BREAD ALONE

Not By Bread Alone is a made-from-scratch bakery that began serving breads and desserts in the early 1980s. In 2001, the business relocated to a larger facility, allowing them to expand their menu and add a café. They offer delicious loaves of bread, soups, unique sandwiches, and pasta salads. The café is named after Deuteronomy 8:3, a verse in the Bible that begins, "Man does not live by bread alone . . ."

Located near the Bay Park Square Mall, Not By Bread Alone makes for a great lunch spot before or after shopping around. The dining space is bright and welcoming. Choose a cold or hot sandwich with a side of soup or salad for a satisfying lunch. One of Not By Bread Alone's specialties is stuffed loaves of bread. These can be custom ordered with savory or sweet fillings. The café is open Monday through Saturday.

940 Hansen Rd., 920-429-9422
notbybread.com

9

EXPERIENCE SUPPER CLUB CULTURE AT RIVER'S BEND

River's Bend is an upscale Wisconsin supper club with panoramic views of Duck Creek, making it a delightful dinner or Sunday brunch spot. Since 1972, River's Bend has been serving up supper club classics like steak, seafood, pasta dishes, and Friday fish fry. In true supper club fashion, each entrée comes with freshly baked bread, a salad bar, and a choice of sides to enjoy.

On the menu you'll also find the classic supper club homemade ice cream drink options. If you're not in the mood for an ice cream drink, they also have wine, cocktails, mocktails, scotch, and beer selections. With indoor, outdoor, and conservatory seating to choose from, River's Bend is perfect for romantic dinners but can also accommodate larger dinner parties. If you're dining with a group, calling ahead to reserve a table is recommended.

792 Riverview Dr., 920-544-9860
riversbendgb.com

MORE SUPPER CLUBS TO DINE AT

Kropp's Supper Club
4570 Shawano Ave., 920-865-7331
kroppssupperclub.com

Club Chalet
4642 Nicolet Dr., 920-866-2341
clubchaletgb.com

Rock Falls Supper Club
6053 Rock Falls Rd., Luxemburg, 920-866-2638

Ten O One Club
1001 Main St., 920-301-3702
1001.club

Redwood Inn
3230 Main St., 920-863-6315

Long Drive Supper Club
897 Riverdale Dr., Hobart, 920-492-4976

10

SAVOR FRESH ITALIAN PASTA DISHES
AT ANGELINA'S

Angelina's Ristorante Authentico Italiano is the place to go for the freshest pasta in the area. Its upstairs seating with a romantic candlelit atmosphere is a draw for date night visitors. Angelina's opened in 1998 and has been serving the area for over 25 years, providing an authentic Italian restaurant experience. Angelina's has been awarded "Best Italian Restaurant in Green Bay" five times by the community-choice Best of the Bay Awards.

Angelina's is a mini-escape to Italy every time you walk through the door. In the warmer months, patio seating is available. With vines and cast-iron tables and chairs, you feel like you're in an Italian villa courtyard. Savory menu items at Angelina's include antipasti, salad, and pasta dishes. Dessert options include cannoli, gelato, and tiramisu. All the desserts are simply scrumptious.

117 N Adams St., 920-437-7248
angelinagb.com

GET FISH AND CHIPS
AT ST. BRENDAN'S INN AND PUB

St. Brendan's Inn is located downtown and offers boutique lodging and authentic Irish cuisine. The pub offers classic Irish dishes such as fish and chips, shepherd's pie, sautéed mussels, and their famous Guinness pot roast. While they have many delicious items on their menu, the fish and chips come highly recommended. The dish is served in a newspaper-print-lined basket, giving it an extra fun presentation, similar to a "chipper" or chip shop experience in Ireland.

With Irish hospitality, meals are served up in a striking pub-style dining room. Dark wood, Irish proverbs, a charming fireplace, and beautiful stained-glass windows make the space feel uniquely Irish. The pub has 15 imported beers on tap, and if you're an Irish whiskey or Scotch whisky aficionado, they have a two-page list of more than 30 imported spirits to choose from. This is the perfect place to enjoy an Irish coffee.

234 S Washington St., 920-884-8484
saintbrendansinn.com

TIP

St. Brendan's is the perfect spot for Friday-night fish fry, a dining tradition in Wisconsin. Stay overnight in one of their 28 guest rooms and get a made-to-order omelet in the morning. Also, during dinner, you should try the curry chips!

DELIGHT IN A FROZEN TREAT

FROM ZESTY'S FROZEN CUSTARD & GRILL

Frozen custard is an incredibly popular dessert in Wisconsin. While similar to ice cream, frozen custard includes egg yolks, which makes the consistency creamier and helps the treat stay colder longer. Zesty's Frozen Custard has been a local favorite for over 35 years and makes its custard fresh daily.

The key to their quality custard is using fresh ingredients and specialty frozen-custard machines that are made in Milwaukee, Wisconsin, by Leon's Frozen Custard. Zesty's sources its ingredients locally whenever possible with their tasty toppings coming from local businesses including Seroogy's and Uncle Mike's Bake Shoppe.

When walking into either of their two locations, you can expect to find a retro-style interior with bright pops of pink, purple, and teal, bringing smiles to those waiting for their orders. If you're looking for a sweet treat, Zesty's is the place to go year-round for fresh, creamy frozen custard.

508 Greene Ave., 920-884-0505
zestyscustard.com

TIP

Check the flavor of the day! Zesty's has a unique flavor showcased each day.

13

GRAB A SLICE
AT RUSTIQUE PIZZERIA + LOUNGE

Rustique Pizzeria is a local favorite pizza spot in a 122-year-old chapel in downtown Suamico. Since opening, they've had to expand their dining space and add a second oven to serve their hungry, loyal fans. Since it's a popular place, if you plan to visit with a group, you'll want to make reservations ahead of time.

Rustique is perfect for romantic date nights or fun family nights out. You'll enjoy an elevated dining space, choose from 17 different kinds of wood-fired pizzas, and indulge in tapas dishes to share at the table. If you're not sure of what to order, a favorite is the sausage and basil pizza, and it will not disappoint. If you're not feeling pizza, they also make a great Cuban sandwich. When dining at the restaurant, and weather permitting, you can choose between indoor or patio dining, which can be delightful on a summer day.

13201 Velp Ave., 920-544-9379
rustiquegb.com

14

DINE BY THE WATERFRONT
AT HAGEMEISTER PARK

Hagemeister Park is a restaurant and bar named after the first field the Green Bay Packers played on in 1919 as a semipro team and for two years after joining the NFL in 1921. The original Hagemeister Park was a community meeting and gathering space. That's exactly what the current-day Hagemeister aims to be.

The restaurant is located along the CityDeck with a 4,000-square-foot outdoor patio filled with people throughout the summer enjoying the weather and the waterfront. In the colder months, the patio has outdoor firepits and heated riverside igloos that can be reserved in advance. Hagemeister Park serves steak, sandwiches, salads, flatbreads, burgers, and wings. On Fridays, Hagemeister Park offers a seafood menu, making this a great spot for Friday-night fish fry, a tradition in Wisconsin.

325 N Washington St., 920-884-9909
hagemeisterpark.com

EAT DIRT

DIRT is a local clean juicery with a mission to provide nutrient-packed, cold-pressed juice and organic food for busy, on-the-go lifestyles. The menu items were created by nutritionists and perfected by chefs. DIRT serves up juices, handcrafted smoothie bowls, grab-and-go foods, and wellness shots. The juicery interior is naturally bright and modern with a cold case for customers to select items to go, a counter to order smoothies and bowls, and a section that showcases some clean products from local small businesses.

There are up to 22 juices to select from, with popular juices called Brainade, carrot pineapple, and Iron Man. If you need a caffeine fix, order the organic mushroom coffee infused with lion's mane or the cold-brew coffee. The juicery is dairy-free-friendly, offering menu items with almond, coconut, and cashew milks. DIRT is open Monday through Saturday and has two locations.

303 Bay Park Sq., Ste. 201D, 920-544-4086
2304 Lineville Rd., Ste. 108, 920-770-4147
dirtcleanjuicery.com

TIP

The key lime green tea smoothie bowl is a personal favorite along with the elderberry pear wellness shot. If you're not sure what to get, ask for a recommendation at the counter. The smoothie artists always have great recommendations!

16

SAMPLE BREWS
AT BADGER STATE BREWING

Badger State Brewing began in 2013 and was the first brewery to open in the Stadium District. It was started by three friends who enjoyed home-brewing together and who appreciated the culture of craft beer and its ability to bring people together. Badger State's commitment to bringing people together has made them a pillar in the community. While at Badger State enjoying a drink, you can sign up for a brewery tour, hang out in the taproom, or soak up the sun in the beer garden.

Throughout the year you can find events from live music in the beer garden to yoga classes in the Barrel Haus, which is the event space attached to the brewery facilities. If you or someone in your group doesn't drink craft beer, you'll be happy to know they have expanded into making delicious hard seltzers, hard cider, and other nonalcoholic drinks.

990 Tony Canadeo Run, 920-634-5687
badgerstatebrewing.com

OTHER PLACES TO ENJOY CRAFT BEER

Titletown Brewing Company
320 N Broadway, 920-437-2337
titletownbrewing.com

Zambaldi Beer
1649 S Webster Ave., 920-455-0473
zambaldi.com

Ahnapee Brewery
1824 Parkfield Ct., Suamico, 920-785-0895
ahnapeebrewery.com

Copper State Brewing Co.
313 Dousman St., 920-489-8575
copperstate.beer

Hinterland Brewery & Restaurant
1001 Lombardi Ave., 920-438-8050
hinterlandbeer.com

Noble Roots Brewing Company
2790 University Ave., 920-489-2874
noblerootsbrewing.com

Stillmank Brewing Co.
215 N Henry St., 920-785-2337
stillmankbrewing.com

Cocoon Brewing Company
2233 Kaftan Way, De Pere, 920-425-4888
cocoonbrewing.com

Crown & Common
1139 Main St., 920-930-1250
crownandcommon.com

17

EXPERIENCE FINE DINING
AT REPUBLIC CHOPHOUSE

Green Bay has many fine dining establishments to choose from, but Republic Chophouse remains at the top of the list for visitors and locals alike. Republic Chophouse offers great food, hospitable service, and an elevated dining atmosphere. The chef focuses on traditional preparations of artisan-aged beef and maintains an ever-changing menu of entrées from lamb to seafood. Republic Chophouse is also popular for its "Sides for Two" menu section and oversized desserts that are simply delightful. Highly recommended sides include the garlic mashed potatoes and the sautéed wild mushrooms.

The restaurant interior was designed with balanced space and privacy in mind, making each dining area feel comfortable and luxurious. This makes Republic Chophouse popular for date nights and business dinners. With an eclectic wine list featuring the finest wine producers in the world, whether you're meeting for a drink or dining here, you're sure to impress your dinner guest.

218 N Adams St., 920-430-7900
republicchophouse.com

OTHER FINE DINING RESTAURANTS

á'Bravo
2069 Central Ct., Ste. 77, 920-432-7286
abravobistro.com

Cedar & Sage Grill House
2040 Airport Dr., 920-327-7911
cedarandsagegrill.com

Taverne in the Sky
1950 S Ridge Rd., 920-327-4600
lodgekohler.com/food-drink

Black & Tan Grille
130 E Walnut St., 920-430-7700
blackandtangrille.com

Chives Restaurant
1749 Riverside Dr., Suamico, 920-434-6441
chivesdining.com

Mangiare
121 N Adams St., 920-403-0900
mangiare-greenbay.com

Plae Bistro
1671 Hoffman Rd., Ste. 10, 920-632-7065
plaebistro.com

Chefusion
307 N Broadway, 920-432-2300
chefusion.com

Union Hotel & Restaurant
200 N Broadway, De Pere, 920-336-6131
unionhoteldepere.com

18

SIP WINE
WITH LEDGESTONE WINERY + VINEYARDS

LedgeStone Winery is in Greenleaf on the Niagara Escarpment, a 650-mile ridge of limestone that extends from southeastern Wisconsin to the Door Peninsula. Limestone is the perfect soil in which to grow grapes for wine because limestone drains well when needed and retains water in drought conditions. It gives the wine a bright acidity, and the wines tend to age well. With this knowledge, it makes perfect sense why LedgeStone is so popular for its wines. In addition to the grapes grown in Wisconsin, LedgeStone uses grapes from Minnesota and the West Coast.

When visiting LedgeStone, guests can enjoy wine outdoors or indoors in the ambiance of the cozy dining areas. The menu has fun starters including a classic cheese plate, truffle fries, and a mezze board. Up to 14 wines are available and can be ordered by the glass, bottle, or as a flight.

6381 WI-57, Greenleaf
ledgestonevineyards.xyz

OTHER PLACES TO SIP WINE

Amphora Wine Bar
131 N Broadway, 920-391-5417
amphorawinebar.com

Aardvark Wine Lounge
304 Pine St., 920-264-5195
aardvarkwinelounge.com

von Stiehl Winery
115 Navarino St., Algoma, 920-487-5208
vonstiehl.com

Parallel 44 Vineyard & Winery
N2185 Sleepy Hollow Rd., Kewaunee, 920-388-4400
44wineries.com

Mona Rose Winery
2696 S Packerland Dr., 920-371-2995
monarosewinery.com

Duck Creek Vineyard and Winery
5046 County Rd. R, Denmark, 920-863-2104
duckcreekwine.com

Captain's Walk Winery
345 S Adams St., 920-431-9255
captainswalkwinery.com

Trout Springs Winery
8150 River Rd., Greenleaf, 920-864-7761
troutspringswinery.com

19

CHOOSE FROM 100 BEERS ON TAP
AT NED KELLY'S PUB

Ned Kelly's on Washington Street is known for having 100 beers on tap at any given time. Their beer menu changes weekly, and beers are hand-selected to bring the best beers from around the world to visitors. Ned Kelly's is open daily, and each beer is ensured to be served at its optimal temperature.

Ned Kelly's carries local, domestic, and international beers. If you're a beer fanatic, this place has any type of beer you might be looking for. They have American ales, Belgian styles, bocks, brown ales, ciders, dark lagers, India pale ales, malted beers, meads, hybrid beers, nitro beers, pilsners, pale lagers, porters, stouts, sours, Scottish-style ales, wheat beers, hard seltzers, wine options, and more. You're sure to find something you like here if you're a beer enthusiast.

223 N Washington St., 920-433-9306
nedkellyspub.com

ORDER TACOS AND MARGARITAS

AT MEXICO LINDO

If you're a fan of Mexican food, Mexico Lindo needs to be on your list of restaurants to try in Green Bay. The family-owned restaurant opened in 2020 after closing their previous restaurant that operated in De Pere for several years. Mexico Lindo has quickly become an area favorite. Focused on high-quality food and service, they provide a superb dining experience. The owners bring culinary expertise to the area from Las Lomas, Jalisco, Mexico.

The restaurant interior is brightly colored, its walls covered with beautiful paintings by a Wisconsin muralist. In the summer, patio seating is available. The Mexico Lindo menu is extensive, offering enchiladas, chimichangas, quesadillas, fajitas, burritos, tacos, and salads. The restaurant offers seafood, pork, chicken, steak, and vegetarian options. The restaurant is popular for its margarita towers, to-go margaritas, and unique tequilas. Chips and salsa are served, and guests can order guacamole that is made fresh tableside.

445 Cardinal Ln., 920-544-0259

21

DINE
AT BLEU RESTAURANT & LOUNGE

Located in De Pere, Bleu Restaurant & Lounge serves elevated plates offering lunch and dinner service. The interior is bright and rustic with chic decor giving the space character. The menu offers scratch-made dishes and locally sourced ingredients when possible. Dishes are segmented on the menu into small, medium, and large plate options. Goat cheese curds, charcuterie, and salads are featured as small plates. Medium plates include flatbread, burgers, mussels, and lobster rolls. Beef tenderloin filets, braised pork shank, salmon, and pan-roasted chicken are mouthwatering large plate options. In addition to these, Bleu has lunch and dinner features that are updated regularly to continuously offer unique dining options.

Bleu's curated inventory of wines, spirits, and beers offers a variety of beverage options. Specialty handcrafted cocktails are also available to elevate your dining experience. Bleu Restaurant & Lounge is open from Tuesday to Saturday.

2200 Dickinson Rd., De Pere, 920-347-5000
bleudining.com

TIP

Get a one-of-a-kind, curated meal at Bleu by reserving a five-course chef's tasting. Pricing begins at $100 per person. Talk about a great date night or celebratory dinner!

Historic Meyer Theatre

MUSIC AND ENTERTAINMENT

SUPPORT LOCAL TALENT AND ART

AT THE TARLTON THEATRE

The Tarlton Theatre is an Art Deco cinema and performing arts center with bars and a restaurant on site. It was originally built in 1924–25 as an automobile dealership before being converted into a theater in 1941. The theater switched hands many times and has been known as the West Theater, West Pitcher Show, and Historic West Theatre. From 2005 the theater sat empty until it was reopened in 2018 as the Tarlton Theatre with considerable renovations completed by owners Tarlton Knight and Mark Mariucci.

The Tarlton Theatre showcases dance, art, music, and film from talented local artists. Popular events include the Tarlton's Art War, Saturday Morning Cartoon Brunch, and Retro Movie Replays played on the theater's original screen. The Tarlton is on the National Register of Historic Places, and the Historic West Fund is a nonprofit committed to preserving and restoring the theater for future generations.

405–409 W Walnut St., 920-562-5612
thetarlton.com

TIP

Plan your visit to the theater during the Tarlton's Art War, the Green Bay Film Festival, or the Bay Area Music Awards to see local artists being showcased! Most of the events at the Tarlton have food or drink specials that are themed around the event taking place.

23

CATCH A SHOW
AT THE WEIDNER CENTER

The Edward W. Weidner Center is a performing arts center that consists of the Cofrin Family Hall, Fort Howard Hall, Jean Weidner Theatre, a dance studio, and a grand foyer. Cofrin Family Hall is the largest theater venue with 2,021 seats. The Weidner Center is on the University of Wisconsin–Green Bay campus and showcases student music, theater, dance, community events, and performances by touring artists and companies. Popular performances include comedians, Broadway musicals, and the Weidner Philharmonic.

Throughout the center, art is displayed in various forms including sculpture, paintings, and textiles. Another feature of the center is the 3,702-pipe Wood Family Organ. Visitors to the Weidner can attend an event or performance or request a tour of the center. The Weidner Center uses digital ticket scanning. Tickets can be digital or printed with the option to be retrieved from will-call at the box office.

2420 Nicolet Dr., 920-465-2400
weidnercenter.com

24

LOOK FOR MURALS
IN THE BROADWAY DISTRICT

The Broadway District is the area to go looking for public art. Broadway is home to more than 35 murals, 10 sculptures, and a variety of other public art displays including painted benches and traffic barriers. Public art can be so powerful in displaying community values, questioning societal assumptions, or transforming and beautifying areas around the city. Murals in the Broadway District do just that. Mural themes include uplifting the community, positive human interaction, imagination, sharing of culture, courage, appreciation of nature, local history, and more.

While wandering the streets in search of murals can be a fun way to spend the day, Downtown Green Bay hosts a website that shows public art on a map, helping visitors locate specific murals they are interested in seeing. This website also identifies the artists and shares their inspiration for creating the mural. To search the public art map, check out the website below.

downtowngreenbay.com/visit/publicart/murals

25

CATCH AN IMPROV SHOW

AT COMEDYCITY THEATRE

ComedyCity is an improv comedy troupe with 30 performers and a theater in De Pere. Each weekend they host shows open to the public on Friday and Saturday. These shows typically involve eight performers. The ComedyCity troupe has been performing since 1987 and has accumulated over 400 alumni. ComedyCity Theatre welcomes guests of all ages and offers a family show and a grown-up show.

When attending a show, I recommend you arrive 30 minutes ahead of time to select a seat, get settled, and order any refreshments. There is a theater bar but there are no drink minimums. If you're new to the improv world, you may be hesitant to interact with the performers. At ComedyCity, you are not required to participate in the show, but they hope to make you feel comfortable enough that you want to join in on the fun.

365 Main Ave., Ste. E, De Pere, 920-345-2600
comedycity.net

WANDER ABOUT
ALL BANDS ON DECK

All Bands on Deck is Green Bay's biggest live music festival featuring more than 100 live local bands and songwriters at over 20 different bars, restaurants, and food trucks throughout the Shipyard District, an area along the Fox River including South Broadway and State Street. Food and drink specials are featured at participating businesses throughout the event. The event is free to attend with no admission or cover charges to enter participating businesses.

SafeRide Shuttles operate during the event and are provided by the Brown County Tavern League to help attendees get from place to place safely. SafeRide is a program that gives patrons a free ride if they can't safely drive home, from any establishment that is a Tavern League of Wisconsin member. The program aims to eliminate drunk driving in Wisconsin and is funded by surcharges on operating while intoxicated (OWI) convictions.

shipyarddistrict.org/all-bands-on-deck

EXPERIENCE THE NIGHTLIFE
ON WASHINGTON STREET AT LOCAL BARS

When it comes to nightlife, Washington Street is incredibly lively. Whether you're looking for easy parking, walkability, dancing, live music, or a place with a laid-back atmosphere, Washington Street has it all. Centrally located parking lots and ramps make this area easy to navigate and walk from place to place.

If you're looking to spin around the dance floor, Black Saddle Tavern & Oasis hosts live music frequently and Stir-Ups Parlor & Saloon has an in-house DJ playing music. Both Kittner's and the Nines have outdoor patios that are especially great in the summer. The Nines serves up craft beer and cocktails while Kittner's has beers on tap and caters to college crowds. The Rabbit Hole is a 1980s–'90s rock and throwback bar with a red and blue neon atmosphere. If you enjoy old-school pinball and retro arcade games, you'll want to stop at Player 2 Arcade Bar.

TIP

While Green Bay has been identified as the "Drunkest City in America" by the *World Population Review* for many years, it is important to note that the reason Green Bay tops the list is due to the percentage of alcohol-related accidents that take place in the city. While you are exploring Washington Street and enjoying the nightlife, be sure to have a designated driver to make sure everyone gets home safely!

WASHINGTON STREET BARS TO CHECK OUT

Black Saddle Tavern & Oasis
201 N Washington St., 920-323-6575
blacksaddletavernandoasis.com

Stir-Ups Parlor & Saloon
125 S Washington St., 920-593-3933

The Nines
121 S Washington St., 920-403-0306

Kittner's
129 S Washington St., 920-433-9187

The Rabbit Hole
209 N Washington St., 920-857-2534

Player 2 Arcade Bar
219 N Washington St., 920-301-3001

VISIT
BAY BEACH AMUSEMENT PARK

Bay Beach Amusement Park is a seasonal park that operates from May to September. Bay Beach offers a variety of rides including kiddie rides, family rides, and thrill rides. One of the most popular rides is the Zippin Pippin. There are more than 20 rides to choose from and each ticket only costs 25 cents. The number of tickets required varies from one to four, depending on the ride. Parking at Bay Beach and admission to the park are always free.

Bay Beach is a popular location to picnic, but watch out for seagulls when you are setting up and eating your meal. If you don't fancy a picnic, vendors sell hot food, snacks, ice cream, and drinks throughout the park. Near the picnic area, there are swings and a playground for families to enjoy. A fun activity for the whole family is riding the train around the park!

1313 Bay Beach Rd., 920-448-3365
greenbaywi.gov/445/bay-beach

TIP

If you're looking for something to do after visiting Bay Beach and feel the need for speed, Kastle Karts is nearby. Kastle Karts is a quarter-mile-long go-kart track that is open May through September. Find more information at kastlekarts.com.

ATTEND
THE ANNUAL ONEIDA POW WOW

A powwow is a gathering hosted by Native American and First Nations communities that usually involves socializing, dancing, singing, and honoring their culture. The Oneida Nation hosts the Oneida Pow Wow each summer. The powwow is open to the public and offers an opportunity to learn about the Oneida culture.

Events and activities that take place during this event include a four-on-four Ojibwe-style traditional lacrosse tournament, a variety of dance and singing competitions, drum contests, and other special events. Most events are incentivized with the opportunity for participants to win prize money. Throughout the event, there are food and craft vendors selling homemade and handmade goods. The event typically lasts three days and tickets can be purchased in advance. Dates and details of the Oneida Pow Wow may change from year to year but updated information can always be found at the website below.

920-496-5647
exploreoneida.com

30

WATCH A PERFORMANCE
AT THE MEYER THEATRE

In 1930 the Meyer Theatre, then known as the FOX Theatre, opened its doors to welcome the public. The theater changed hands in 1932 and again in 1978. In 1998 a group of community leaders came together to save the theater, which was at risk of being torn down. They received generous donations to renovate and rename it the Robert T. Meyer Theatre, reopening to the public in 2002.

Over the years, the theater has hosted star performers including Nat King Cole, Louis Armstrong, the Miller Brothers, the Beach Boys, and Johnny Cash. The interior is breathtakingly ornate, resembling the Spanish gardens of Seville with Mediterranean-influenced adornments. The Mighty Wurlitzer pipe organ, one of the few left in working order anywhere in the country, is still used today. Hosting 180 to 200 performances annually, with a capacity of 1,011, the Meyer Theatre welcomes over 80,000 guests per year.

117 S Washington St., 800-895-0071
meyertheatre.org

PLAY
AT THE CHILDREN'S MUSEUM OF GREEN BAY

The Children's Museum of Green Bay has been serving the community for over 34 years. Three core values the museum focuses on are developing foundational skills, respecting childhood, and lighting a creative spark for lifelong learning. Hands-on play and exploration are at the center of everything the museum does, from its exhibits to programming. Children and adults can connect through play in a variety of activities at the museum.

The museum functions as a town square of sorts with exhibits like the farmers market, the fire station, the diner, the vet clinic, the auto garage, and more. This format allows children to explore, create, face fears, and develop confidence in the world around them. Weekly programming activity options include Creativity Station, Bilingual Storytime, Growing Strong, and Messy Art. In addition to regular programming, the museum hosts summer, spring, and winter break camps. The museum is open from Tuesday to Sunday.

1230 Bay Beach Rd., 920-432-4397
gbchildrensmuseum.org

JOIN AN ARTIST WORKSHOP AT THE ART GARAGE

The Art Garage is a creative hub that opened in 2006 and aims to make art accessible to the public. The Art Garage is on the east side of Green Bay in a 100-year-old former canning factory made of Cream City brick, a creamy light-colored brick made from clay around Milwaukee, Wisconsin. Inside the historic space, there are artist studios, gallery space, and multipurpose spaces used for events. Throughout the year there are art vendor markets, parties, arts organizations meetings, workshops, and classes.

The Art Garage has a casual welcoming atmosphere, and it is always free for the public to visit. The works of artists displayed in the gallery space range from amateur to professional skill levels. The workshops the Art Garage hosts throughout the year are excellent opportunities to try something new or refine skills in a welcoming environment. A variety of workshops are offered, from drawing to ceramics. The workshop schedule can be viewed on the Art Garage website and is updated each season with new class offerings.

1400 Cedar St., 920-448-6800
theartgarage.org

33

EXPLORE
THE NEW ZOO

Open year-round, the NEW Zoo is a must-see for families visiting the area. The zoo has a variety of animals to observe and learn about—from native species of Wisconsin, like deer, badgers, and bobcats, to animals from around the world, such as penguins, lions, and giraffes. The children's zoo area has farm animals like goats and chickens near one of the two playground areas. A unique experience that the NEW Zoo offers is the opportunity to feed giraffes from a tall platform, allowing visitors to get close to the animals.

The NEW Zoo has a picnic area situated just before the entrance and near the Mayan Restaurant within the zoo that serves snacks and meals for visitors. On the grounds, you'll also find the zoo train and a gift shop. The NEW Zoo hosts fun events throughout the year for the public like Zoo Boo and EggStravaganZoo.

4378 Reforestation Rd., 920-434-7841
newzoo.org

TIP

After visiting the zoo, check out Vickery Village. The village is made up of historically significant buildings to Suamico that have been restored. You'll find delightful shops and fantastic places to eat like Chives Restaurant or Spork Cafe. Grab ice cream from Suamico Creamery!

34

GET YOUR GROOVE ON
AT THAT 70'S BAR

That 70's Bar is a groovy spot on Broadway that welcomes patrons with bright colors, lava lamps, giant Twister on the wall, and hula hoops on the dance floor. The bar was opened by co-owners Brian Bunkelman and Chris Hansen, who also own the Sardine Can a couple of doors down. Their motivations were to bring a smile to people's faces, make the space entertaining, and keep people wanting to come back.

The bottom of the bar itself is made to look like the Partridge Family's bus. References to *Scooby-Doo*, John Travolta, *The Brady Bunch*, and Flower Power give the bar a strong sense of nostalgia. Music played in the bar is from the 1960s to the '90s with hits from ABBA, Cher, the Monkees, and more. A funky sign in the bar reads "Be groovy or go home," which gives the bar an even stronger sense of character and fun.

124 S Broadway

INDULGE IN A SPA SERVICE
AT KOHLER WATERS SPA

The Kohler Waters Spa is within Lodge Kohler and is designed to treat the mind, body, and soul. It offers specialty massages, hydrotherapy, body treatments, facials, nails, lash and brow treatments, waxing services, salon appointments, reiki, and other holistic services.

Along with spa services, guests can enjoy the spa amenities including a sauna, steam room, and cool plunge pool. It is recommended that you arrive at least 30 minutes prior to your appointment to check in and optimize your time to relax before your service. To ensure the spa is a safe, welcoming, and quiet space, phones and other devices are prohibited in the locker rooms, treatment rooms, and relaxation areas. The boutique on-site carries a selection of hair- and skin-care items from the spa. The spa's signature Hollyhock scent is available in body-care products in the boutique.

1950 S Ridge Rd., 855-395-7638
lodgekohler.com

VIEW LOCAL ART
AT ARTFEST

ArtFest is exactly what it sounds like: a festival of art. This free event takes place annually in downtown Green Bay. For a couple of days, the streets are filled with live music, art, food, demonstrations, and activities. ArtFest not only brings joy and creativity to the area; it supports projects in the downtown districts like murals, art installations, and beautification.

ArtFest provides the perfect opportunity to find a new piece of art for your home or office space. Art mediums available include paintings, sculptures, photography, mixed-media pieces, and more. When you purchase a piece of art at ArtFest, you are directly supporting local artists! Activities at the event allow attendees to get creative and participate in a variety of art forms. Local vendors and food trucks serve up culinary art from diverse cuisines that delights ArtFest foodies.

downtowngreenbay.com/artfest

37

TAKE A TOUR
OF PARADISE NORTH DISTILLERY

Tour Paradise North Distillery to learn from a family-owned business about the process of spirit making. Paradise North opened as an artisan distillery in 2021, manufacturing and selling premium handcrafted, full-bodied spirits. The distillery produces rums, whiskeys, gin, and vodka. Located on Bay Beach Road near the South Bay Marina, it's easy to imagine paradise, especially when sipping the Beach Road Spiced or Blackstrap Rum.

While at the distillery, visitors can take a tour of the distilling process, do a spirit sampling, or try one of their 25 handcrafted signature cocktails. With more than 10 spirits to sample, the customizable flights of four spirits are popular among visitors. In addition to spirits, the Paradise North Distillery serves mocktails, sodas, and juices as nonalcoholic options. Charcuterie boards, dips, chips, and soft pretzels can be ordered as well.

101 Bay Beach Rd., Ste. 5, 920-328-9949
paradisenorthdistillery.com

Lambeau Field

SPORTS AND RECREATION

CHANT "GO PACK GO!"
AT LAMBEAU FIELD DURING A PACKERS GAME

Green Bay is the smallest city to have a professional sports team in the United States. In the early days of the National Football League, other small-town teams faded away but our team continued. Football has shaped what Green Bay is today, and the heart of our city is Lambeau Field. It's been home to the Packers since 1957 and is the second-oldest stadium in use by an NFL team. Game days in Green Bay are electric. You can feel the energy across the city as our fans and players get ready for the main event: kickoff. There is no better way to connect with this city than to chant "Go Pack Go!" with us at Lambeau Field.

Plan for your game-day experience at packers.com, where you can view the team schedule, ticket purchasing details, and game-day-specific information.

1265 Lombardi Ave., 920-569-7500
packers.com

TIP

Don't forget to stop in the Packers Pro Shop while you're at Lambeau Field to stock up on Packers gear! If you're visiting in July or early August, see if you're in town for Training Camp or Family Night, which are both opportunities to see the Packers preparing for the season.

OBSERVE WILDLIFE
AT THE BAY BEACH WILDLIFE SANCTUARY

The Bay Beach Wildlife Sanctuary is a 600-acre urban wildlife refuge that opened in 1936 as a waterfowl rehabilitation site. It has since expanded to include animal exhibits, educational displays, hiking trails, wildlife viewing and photography opportunities, and a wildlife rehabilitation center. The rehabilitation center and the sanctuary care for more than 6,000 orphaned and injured animals annually. Visitors can observe a variety of species in the sanctuary including wolves, deer, bobcats, turtles, owls, otters, snakes, birds of prey, and more.

There is no admission, and the sanctuary is open year-round. Hundreds and thousands of bird-watchers, families, and wildlife enthusiasts visit each year to explore the sanctuary and observe its inhabitants. A favorite interactive activity at the Bay Beach Wildlife Sanctuary is feeding the waterfowl. Whole corn can be purchased in the observation building while visiting. Another favored activity is watching the feeding of the wolves each day.

1660 E Shore Dr., 920-391-3671
baybeachwildlife.com

CROSS-COUNTRY SKI
AT THE BROWN COUNTY REFORESTATION CAMP

The E.J. "Ollie" Smith Reforestation Camp in Brown County is 1,500 acres of nature to explore in Suamico near the NEW Zoo and Adventure Park. In the winter, trails are groomed, making it a great destination to cross-country ski, snowshoe, fat-tire bike, and snowmobile. There are 19 miles of trails designated for skiing at the reforestation camp with three miles of the trails lit for skiing in the evening.

Skis are available for rent from the adventure park next to the ski lodge at the reforestation camp. Snowshoes and bikes are also available for rent. The ski lodge overlooks a beautiful wooded area and is open to skiers, snowshoers, and snowmobilers throughout the winter as a warming shelter. The reforestation camp also has 51 all-season sites that accommodate RVs, campers, and tents.

4418 Reforestation Rd., Suamico, 920-448-6242

TIP

Visit the reforestation camp in the summer too! Activities like hiking, fishing, picnicking, mountain biking, and horseback riding are popular summer activities at the reforestation camp.

PICK APPLES
AT THE ONEIDA NATION APPLE ORCHARD

The Oneida Nation Apple Orchard spans approximately 40 acres and contains around 4,000 trees. The orchard offers more than 20 varieties of apples and other produce, such as strawberries, raspberries, blackberries, sweet corn, squash, and pumpkins, depending on the season.

A visit to the apple orchard can be to pick up a bushel of prepicked apples or to pick your own. In Wisconsin, pick-your-own farms are incredibly popular, and depending on the season, within a short drive from Green Bay, you can visit a farm and pick blueberries, strawberries, sweet or tart cherries, pumpkins, and more. Apples are typically ready to be picked between August and October, but you'll want to reach out and confirm apple-picking dates. Each apple variety has its own optimal picking time frame, so this is very dependent on the farm or orchard you are visiting.

3976 W Mason St., Oneida, 920-869-2468
exploreoneida.com

TIP

Each September, the Oneida Nation hosts Big Apple Fest as a way to invite the community to celebrate the harvest and learn about the Oneida Nation. Festival activities include tours of an Oneida longhouse, barrel-racing demonstrations, a petting zoo, pick-your-own apples, an apple pie baking contest, live music, and wagon rides.

WALK
THE FOX RIVER STATE TRAIL

If you're looking for a great trail to check out in the area, you'll want to hop on the Fox River State Trail. It's 25 miles long and follows the Fox River through Brown County. The trail begins at the base of Green Bay downtown then follows the river going south. The first 11 miles of the trail are paved, making it easily accessible for strollers, bikes, rollerblades, and wheelchairs. The remainder of the trail is crushed gravel.

Along the trail you'll get views of downtown Green Bay, CityDeck, and downtown De Pere before hitting the gravel. From there you'll enjoy lovely nature scenes along the river. If you plan to bike or skate the path, you will need to get a Wisconsin State Trail Pass. The 11 miles of paved trail in Brown County are plowed and maintained throughout the winter so this trail can be used year-round.

920-448-4466
dnr.wisconsin.gov/topic/parks/foxriver

TIP

The Fox River State Trail is pet-friendly, so if you're traveling with a pet, this is a great way to get a nice long walk in! Pets must always be on leashes 8 feet or shorter.

TAILGATE
ON GAME DAY

Make the most of your game day at Lambeau Field by participating in the time-honored tradition of tailgating. Tailgating is a social gathering where a meal is served out of the back of a vehicle, typically in a stadium parking lot. At Lambeau Field, you can tailgate a couple of different ways. First is the traditional format, which can be achieved by grilling brats or burgers behind the vehicle you drove to Lambeau Field. There isn't a formal process for tailgating; just show up, park in an open spot, and let tailgating begin. Tailgaters are welcomed in parking lots around Lambeau Field on game day but tailgating ends at kickoff.

The alternative options are to visit the Johnsonville Tailgate Village or Stadium View Sports Bar. Both are near Lambeau Field and offer a fun, festive environment in which to hang out before and during the game. Food and drink can be purchased inside.

Lambeau Field
Lot 1, S Oneida St., 920-569-7500
packers.com

Johnsonville Tailgate Village
1265 Lombardi Ave., 920-569-7148
packers.com/lambeau-field/
johnsonville-tailgate-village

Stadium View Sports Bar
1963 Holmgren Way, 920-498-1989
thestadiumview.com

44

CATCH
A GREEN BAY ROCKERS BASEBALL GAME

The Green Bay Rockers are part of the Northwoods League, which is one of the premier summer collegiate baseball leagues in the country. This league is an opportunity for players to display their talents to professional scouts. The team has been around since 2007 and has recently gone through a name change under new ownership. From the Green Bay Booyah they were renamed the Green Bay Rockers. The aim of the name change was to incorporate live music to enhance the fan experience at games. Along with live music, there are concessions and fun activities for families.

You can catch a Rockers game May through August at Capital Credit Union Park. Tickets can be purchased online or on arrival if there are tickets available. Children 5 and under are allowed to attend for free. Gates open 60 minutes before the game, and that is when the pregame concert begins!

2231 Holmgren Way, 920-497-7225
northwoodsleague.com/green-bay-rockers

TIP

In honor of the Friday night fish fry tradition in Wisconsin, whenever the Rockers play on Friday nights, they play as the "Supper Clubbers"—another nod to Wisconsin culture.

EXPLORE
BARKHAUSEN WATERFOWL PRESERVE

With over 900 acres of forest, meadows, and wetlands to explore, the L. H. Barkhausen Waterfowl Preserve is a wonderful place to spend a day. There are over nine miles of hiking trails through the preserve that take you through marshes and forests, allowing you to observe the variety of wildlife, waterfowl, and plant species. The West Shores Interpretive Center has hands-on exhibits and offers educational programming throughout the year for visitors.

Barkhausen Waterfowl Preserve is home to Sensory Woods, which connects people with all abilities to the sensations of nature. The park staff envisioned the project, and support for community organizations brought the project to life. There are a chime wall, a raised wildflower bed, interactive stations, scattered seating areas, and accessible trails. These additions allow visitors to have a more immersive experience. The preserve also has an all-terrain battery-powered wheelchair that can be reserved by visitors for free.

2024 Lakeview Dr., Suamico, 920-448-4466
browncountywi.gov/community/parks-department/general-information/barkhausen-waterfowl-preserve

TIP

If you plan to visit in the winter, there are snowshoeing trails and cross-country ski trails to enjoy!

HAVE A BLAST
AT THE TUNDRA LODGE WATERPARK

The Tundra Lodge is a hotel with the largest water park in the area. It's incredibly popular among families and on Lombardi Avenue, not far from Lambeau Field. The water park is 30,000 square feet with 500 feet of waterslides, an aquatic playground, and the area's only lazy river. No matter the season, you can enjoy and warm up in the indoor/outdoor whirlpools.

Water park passes are included when you stay at the Tundra Lodge, but day passes are available for visitors and locals. If you're just visiting for the day, there are lockers near the water park as well. When you get tired of swimming, the Gold Rush Arcade is nearby with more than 70 arcade games to play. There is always something fun to do at the Tundra Lodge!

865 Lombardi Ave., 920-405-8700
tundralodge.com/water-park-arcade

ICE FISH
ON THE BAY

Ice fishing is a popular winter pastime in Green Bay, and the state of Wisconsin is actually one of the best places to ice fish in the United States. Green Bay is a basin of Lake Michigan and is home to the largest walleyes in the state. In addition to walleyes, Green Bay whitefish are also plentiful. Where there is good fishing, you can bet there are good fishing guides and charters. There are a variety of companies to help you catch the fish of your dreams while visiting Green Bay.

If you're a pro and want to bring your own supplies and skills to Green Bay, you can sign up to compete in a fishing tournament hosted on the Fox River or on Green Bay. If you plan on ice fishing, make sure you get a fishing license ahead of time.

dnr.wisconsin.gov/topic/fishing

48

GOLF
THORNBERRY CREEK
AT ONEIDA

Thornberry Creek at Oneida is a public golf course right outside of Green Bay that offers 27 holes of championship golf. Public golf courses are common in Wisconsin and great because they welcome all golfers to play at the course instead of requiring a golfer to be a member. The Legends and Iroquois courses are two Rick Jacobson–designed courses containing sloping hills and pristine Northwoods scenery that provide challenging yet enjoyable golf.

Thornberry Creek at Oneida is the official golf course of the Green Bay Packers and in 2019 hosted the Thornberry Creek LPGA Classic Tournament. Golfers of all ages and abilities are welcome at Thornberry Creek, and it's recommended that golfers book tee times seven days in advance to ensure availability. Proper golf attire is required by all guests, and each paid greens fee includes a small bucket of range balls.

4470 N Pine Tree Rd., Oneida, 920-434-7501
golfthornberry.com

49

PICNIC
AT PAMPERIN PARK

Beautifully landscaped and providing serene views, Pamperin Park is the perfect place for an afternoon picnic. From picnic tables to grassy areas, there are options throughout the park for where to set up your picnic. Duck Creek slowly flows by, cutting the park into halves. There's a beautiful suspension bridge that reconnects both sides of the park for visitors to wander across.

Pamperin Park is the largest developed park in the Brown County park system. With 10,000 square feet of formal gardens, volleyball courts, a 17,000-square-foot playground, and an 18-hole disc golf course, there is no surprise why it's such a popular destination for couples and families to picnic and spend the afternoon. The park is dog friendly, but they must be on a leash at all times.

2801 County Rd. RK
browncountywi.gov/community/parks-department/general-information/pamperin-park

50

GO ICE-SKATING AND TUBING
AT TITLETOWN

Titletown is a vibrant community with tons of fun activities and events year-round, right next to Lambeau Field. In the winter, it's a great place to go ice-skating and tubing. For ice-skating at HyVee Plaza, buy skating passes and rentals in the Admissions building upon arrival. Around the ice rink, you'll find fires lit to warm up around and trees wrapped in twinkling lights.

For tubing on Ariens Hill, Titletown tubes are provided free of charge, but riders must purchase a tubing ticket from the Admissions building. The hill is 46 feet tall and there are two lanes for riders to use. Riders must be at least 42 inches tall, and only one rider is allowed per tube. Safety waivers must be signed before skating or tubing, and Titletown is cashless. 46 Below is a café on site that serves warm drinks and snacks.

1025 Lombardi Ave., 920-569-7500
titletown.com

TIP

Titletown hosts many events and festivals throughout the year, so be sure to check out their event calendar when planning your trip. The most popular events are the free concerts they host before each home game at Lambeau Field. There is so much to do at Titletown!

51

FIND FONFEREK'S GLEN

There is a hidden geographical gem in the area that often surprises visitors. Fonferek's Glen is a unique 75-acre county park, the shining star of which is a 30-foot waterfall surrounded by dolomite cliffs and a stone archway. These geographic wonders are part of the Niagara Escarpment, a 650-mile ridge of limestone that runs through Canada and the US within the Great Lakes region. In Wisconsin, the ridge extends from the Door Peninsula to the southeastern corner of the state.

While visiting the area, be sure to stay on the designated trails as there are steep cliffs, falling rocks, and rugged terrain in this natural conservancy area. The waterfall can easily be viewed from a platform overlook, which makes the beautiful view easily accessible. The park is pet-friendly, but pets must remain on leash while visiting.

2825 Dutchman Rd., 920-448-6242

TIP

Are you chasing waterfalls? Check out Wequiock Falls when driving north on Highway 57 toward Door County.

TRY SKATEBOARDING
AT GBASO

Green Bay Action Sports Organization (GBASO) is a community nonprofit that aims to develop skills in youth, including social, physical, and leadership skills, while providing access to action sports and educational opportunities. GBASO began as the mission of Brian Schroeder to bring a safe indoor skate park to Green Bay for his two young sons and other youth in the area. After a lot of hard work and help from volunteers, the skate park opened to the public in 2014.

They recently relocated to a larger facility in 2023, and the indoor skate park is now one of the largest in the Midwest! GBASO's indoor space is open for a variety of action sports including skateboarding, scootering, BMX, and in-line skating. All ages and abilities are welcome at GBASO. Visitors can join classes and events or come during open park hours. The facility is open seven days a week.

2351 Holmgren Way, Ste. 102, 920-371-6852
gbaso.org

TIP

GBASO has the only skate shop in Brown County. Here you'll find skateboards, skateboarding apparel, and more.

HIT THE BAIRD CREEK TRAILS
TO SEE FALL FOLIAGE

The Baird Creek Greenway is home to 14 miles of trails for hiking, mountain biking, walking, running, and exploring. Hiking the trails is extraordinary in any season; however, fall is one of the most picturesque times to explore the trails. As the cooler weather arrives, the backdrop of the trails turns from bright green to crispy golden and auburn.

One of the trails is categorized as easy with a paved path 1.6 miles in length. Four intermediate trails, ranging from 1.2 to 2 miles each, give great options for those seeking a variety of scenery. The remaining three trails are advanced with one of those specifically being recommended for mountain bikers.

There are four spots to park that allow you to hit the trail right away. Parking is available at Triangle Hill, Christa McAuliffe Park, McKenzie Lane, or the lower parking lot.

500 Beverly Rd.
bairdcreek.org

TIP

In the winter, come back to Triangle Hill and enjoy sledding, skiing, snowboarding, and snowshoeing at the Triangle Sports Area. With tube rentals, tow lifts, and a heated chalet, the Triangle Sports Area is a great place for families to visit in the winter.

HIKE ALONG THE SHORE
AT BAY SHORE COUNTY PARK

Cecil Depeau Bay Shore County Park offers beautiful views of the Bay of Green Bay and is situated on the Niagara Escarpment, which is a geologic formation created 400 million years ago by an ancient sea. The park offers camping, boating, kayaking, hiking, picnicking, playgrounds, and swimming, and it has a public boat launch. There are 1.5 miles of hiking trails at Bay Shore County Park.

The hiking here is fantastic as the trails bring you along the cliffs allowing for a closer look at the rock formations of the Niagara Escarpment. From the trails, you will also find viewpoints where you can see the bay or look down to see the beach. There are paths of stairs that lead down to the beach, and what better way to end a hike than with a swim in Lake Michigan? Sunsets along the beach are exquisite.

5637 Sturgeon Bay Rd., New Franken, 920-448-4466
browncountywi.gov/community/parks-department/general-information/bay-shore-park

TIP

After your hike, head north to Dykesville Bowl for ridiculously good cheese curds!

STROLL
ALONG THE CITYDECK

The CityDeck is a quarter-mile-long riverfront promenade along the Fox River in downtown Green Bay. It's a great area to take a stroll; it's also pet-friendly if you want to take your dog for a walk along the water. Each season, your walk along the CityDeck might be a little different. In the summer, you'll see people out dining on patios and hear live music on Friday nights.

In the winter, you'll see a variety of holiday lights displays, photo ops along the boardwalk, and clear igloos that can be reserved for a unique dining experience. In the fall, you'll see people sitting around the fires on the patio of Hagemeister Park and the colorful leaves on the trees across the river. Spring brings joggers and dog walkers out to enjoy the sunshine that's starting to warm up the area.

301 N Washington St., 920-448-3365
greenbaywi.gov/facilities/facility/details/citydeck-110

CHEER ON
THE GREEN BAY GAMBLERS

If you're into hockey, you need to get tickets to a Green Bay Gamblers game while you're in town. The Gamblers are a junior hockey team in the Eastern Conference of the United States Hockey League (USHL). The team's home rink is in Ashwaubenon at the Resch Center, a 10,000-seat arena. The Gamblers have been around for 30 years and have won two national championships, five Anderson Cups, four Clark Cups, four USHL Eastern Division titles, and a USHL Northern Division title.

Tickets to watch a Gamblers game can be purchased online in advance of the game. During the season, games are themed to add to the fan experience. Popular game themes include family night, bud night, and college night. Going to a game with friends or family makes for a great time!

820 Armed Forces Dr., 800-895-0071
gamblershockey.com

TIP

The Resch Center is a multipurpose arena and hosts concerts, shows, Phoenix men's basketball, and Blizzard indoor football. The Resch Expo, just next door, hosts events and trade shows on a variety of topics from hunting to holiday craft shows. Check out events at the Resch Center and the Resch Expo when you're planning things to do in Green Bay!

57

PUTT-PUTT
AT DUCK CREEK GOLF CENTER

If you're looking for some fun, healthy competition for your family or friends, look no further than Duck Creek Golf Center's miniature golf course. Rushing streams and waterfalls flow throughout the course. At the Duck Creek Golf Center, you'll also find a driving range with 45 hitting stations, nine target greens. and a large putting green. There are beautiful views around the center that provide the perfect backdrop for golf.

After you're finished golfing, stop back by the desk to purchase some ice cream or snacks to enjoy before moving on to your next activity of the day. The Duck Creek Golf Center is open daily seasonally, May to October. Mini golf ends at dusk, and the driving range closes one hour before sunset. The course is open as long as weather permits.

345 Village Ct., 920-498-2797

SWIM
AT JOANNES AQUATIC CENTER

Splash away the heat this summer at the Joannes Aquatic Center. There's fun for the whole family with a tot sand play area, a heated pool with a zero-depth wading area, waterslides, and sand volleyball courts. With 23-foot slides for the daring swimmers and a mini-slide in a shallow pool for the littles, you're sure to please everyone in the family with a day at Joannes Aquatic Center.

The aquatic center is open from mid-June to the end of August. There are lounge chairs, coin-operated lockers, and a concessions stand provided for visitors, so all you need to think about is what you'll wear to swim. Oh, and don't forget to bring a towel! Once you're done at the aquatic center, check out the huge playground and the rest of Joannes Park.

1430 E Walnut St., 920-448-3365

WALK THROUGH
THE GREEN BAY BOTANICAL GARDEN

The Green Bay Botanical Garden opened to the public in 1996 after years of planning and preparation. Today the garden is 47 acres in total with 23 acres developed and the remaining acres undeveloped woodland or wetlands. There are 98,000 plants from Wisconsin and around the world featured in the garden. Over 300,000 bulbs bloom each spring from daffodils to tulips in bright beautiful colors. The conifer reference garden is one of two in the state and the magnolia collection is the first and only nationally accredited garden of its kind in Wisconsin.

The Bell Children's Garden is an awe-inspiring area for children to play and learn while connecting to nature. The garden hosts a variety of events, classes, and exhibits throughout the year so there is always something new to discover. The garden is open year-round and about half of it is paved, with scooters and wheelchairs free to use.

TIP

Come back to the garden in the winter to see the Garden of Lights, a display of 350,000 lights arranged in nature-inspired displays. You can choose to walk along the paths or take a horse-drawn carriage ride. Don't forget to get hot chocolate!

VISIT THE KITTIES
AT SAFE HAVEN PET SANCTUARY

If you're a cat person, a visit to Safe Haven Pet Sanctuary should be at the top of your list! Safe Haven is a nonprofit organization that operates a no-kill, cage-free sanctuary for kittens, cats, dogs, and puppies in any physical or physiological condition. Safe Haven Pet Sanctuary rescues hundreds of animals every year and they operate 100 percent on donations. Safe Haven welcomes visitors to the sanctuary during open hours and hosts fun events like Yoga with Kitties that helps fundraise to care for the animals.

Safe Haven is in the Broadway District, in a white building that has a ton of cats painted around the entrances. If you walk by their building, you'll likely see curious cats sitting in the windows. Their mission is to have "no pet left behind," and they are gracious to those who donate, volunteer, foster, or adopt.

151 N Broadway, 920-489-2462
safehavenpet.org

Historic Hotel Northland

CULTURE AND HISTORY

DISCOVER LOCAL STORIES AND HISTORY

AT THE NEVILLE PUBLIC MUSEUM

With aims of "bringing the world to Green Bay," the Green Bay Art Club began a collection of significant objects in 1915 as a small display in a local library. In 1925 a generous donation allowed for expansion to a standalone building. This donation named the collection the Neville Public Museum, after Green Bay's 25th mayor, Arthur Neville. Today the museum has rotating and permanent displays on history, art, and science. There are two levels of galleries, a gift shop, and a theater.

When visiting, you can expect to see displays showcasing early settlers in Green Bay, the history and impact of the local paper-making industry, highlights of those who have impacted or transformed Northeast Wisconsin, and so much more. Admission for the museum is free for children 2 years and under, military members, and veterans. Discounts are offered to children, seniors, and family members of military members.

210 Museum Pl., 920-448-4460
nevillepublicmuseum.org

62

EXPERIENCE LIVING HISTORY
AT HERITAGE HILL STATE PARK

Heritage Hill State Park is an open-air living-history park. The living-history format allows for education, entertainment, and engagement with authentic historical and cultural displays. Throughout the 56-acre park, history is brought to life by actors interpreting the past to give visitors an insight into life in Wisconsin during the 1600s. The park opened to the public in 1977 and consists of 26 original structures that were reconstructed within the park.

With more than 9,000 artifacts on display, there is plenty to see. Some popular structures to visit include the schoolhouse, the Belgian farmhouse, and the cheese factory. In the warmer months, animals are brought in from local farms, so depending on when you visit, you may get to see chickens, goats, and a dairy cow. The park offers guided walking and tram tours with a coffeehouse and gift shop on site.

2640 S Webster Ave., 920-448-5150
heritagehillgb.org

TIP

An area favorite is visiting Heritage Hill during their holiday season when cookies are baked using historical methods, carolers sing, and fresh snow falls around you.

63

WALK AMONG LEGENDS
AT THE PACKERS HALL OF FAME

The Green Bay Packers Hall of Fame tells the story of the Green Bay Packers, from their origins to the present-day NFL team. Green Bay is the smallest city to have an NFL team and this museum shares how the support of the local community was integral to the long-term success of the team. Inside there are two levels showcasing artifacts from past legends and present players, and fan memorabilia. You'll also get to see trophies won by the team up close and the display of inductees to the Packers Hall of Fame.

The displays throughout are educational and inspirational, sharing the community's love for the team and the dedication of both the Packers and their fans. Even if you aren't a football fan, you need to visit the hall of fame. You'll leave with a new appreciation and understanding of the relationship between the Packers and the Green Bay community.

1265 Lombardi Ave., 920-569-7512
packershofandtours.com

TIP

Pair a visit to the hall of fame with a Lambeau Field Stadium Tour. There are three types of tours you can choose from depending on how much of the stadium you want to see. During the Legendary Tour you get to see the visiting team's locker room, the Lee Remmel Press Box, the player's tunnel, and the sideline.

STAY
AT THE HISTORIC HOTEL NORTHLAND

When Hotel Northland opened in 1924, it was the largest hotel in the state. The hotel took $1 million to build and was designed by Herbert W. Tullgren, a well-known Milwaukee architect. The hotel is known to have hosted many notable guests, an NFL meeting, NFL visiting teams, and the event where Vince Lombardi was formally introduced as coach and general manager of the Packers.

In 1980, the hotel was transformed into housing before closing and sitting empty for 10 years. A $50 million renovation began in 2015. The property reopened in 2019 as an Autograph Collection Hotel with 160 rooms, two restaurants, and a beautifully restored lobby. The Crystal Ballroom, marble steps, pink terrazzo tiles, and star-patterned green and white mosaic tiles are a reminder of the prosperity and glory of the 1920s. Hotel Northland is charming, elegant, and centrally located in Green Bay's downtown.

304 N Adams St., 920-393-7499
marriott.com/en-us/hotels/grbak-hotel-northland-autograph-collection

EAT AL'S HAMBURGERS

Al's Hamburgers has been serving up burgers and shakes since 1934. Customers are welcomed inside the tiny restaurant on Washington Street by a retro neon sign stating EAT. When you step into Al's you'll see retro diner stools, booths, and a classic checkered floor. With over 90 years serving up juicy burgers, this restaurant delights visitors and is a must-visit spot. In 2017, Al's was visited by famous Food Network host Alton Brown, who endorsed the delicious burgers via social media. So, if you don't take my recommendation, take his!

The menu has 10 different burgers to choose from along with eight shake varieties. Before you order, be sure to ask about the shake of the month! Popular sides include french fries, tater tots, onion rings, and, of course, white cheddar Wisconsin cheese curds. Discounts are offered to first responders including police, fire, and military with proof of employment.

131 S Washington St., 920-437-5114
alshamburgergb.com

66

SHOUT "ALL ABOARD!" INSIDE A LOCOMOTIVE
AT THE NATIONAL RAILROAD MUSEUM

The National Railroad Museum was established in 1956 and is one of the largest railroad museums in the nation with 70-plus pieces of rolling stock and more than 100,000 artifacts. This extensive collection is the only congressionally designated national-status railroad museum in the United States.

During a visit to the museum, you can view the gallery displays, a variety of train cars and locomotives, and the Children's Discovery Depot. You can also take a train ride around the museum grounds. The ride takes approximately 25 minutes, and during the journey, the conductor talks about railroad safety and hobo culture, and points out sights along the way. If you're looking for a specific locomotive, caboose, or passenger car, the museum has a detailed map so you can easily navigate the museum and find what you are looking for.

2285 S Broadway, 920-437-7623
nationalrrmuseum.org

67

STAY
AT THE ASTOR HOUSE BED & BREAKFAST, BUILT IN 1888

Built in 1888, the Astor House was owned privately by a number of families until 1993. It was then renovated and converted to the area's first bed-and-breakfast in 1994. There are five cozy guest rooms, each with its own unique theme. The inn is known to be peaceful and welcoming. It is often compared to the Dragonfly Inn from *Gilmore Girls*.

Each day a three-course breakfast is made from scratch and is served to guests by owners Tom and Linda Steber, who purchased the inn in 2019. In addition to a delicious breakfast daily, guests can enjoy Scotty P's Big Mug Coffee, owned by actor Scott Patterson, who plays Luke in *Gilmore Girls*. Linda from the Astor House collaborated with Scott to make Scotty's Biscottis, which are exclusively available at the inn. If you're looking for a quaint, cozy stay, the Astor House is the place.

637 S Monroe Ave., 920-432-3585
astorhouse.com

TIP

Scotty's Biscottis can be preordered for pickup by calling the Astor House in advance. Some flavors available include Dutch chocolate, butterscotch, and English toffee!

LEARN ABOUT ONEIDA CULTURE AND HISTORY
AT THE ONEIDA NATION MUSEUM

The Oneida Nation Museum opened in 1979 to share the history and culture of the Oneida and Iroquois nations. The museum displays begin with the creation story and origins of the native nations. From there you can step into a replica longhouse. The displays are extensive, covering early history to challenges the nation faces today.

Each display in the museum has an interactive feature, either an audio narration or an interactive digital display. One of the coolest things about this museum is the ability to listen to displays in English and Oneida. While visiting the museum, you can also experience the hands-on area, walk through nature trails, visit the Three Sisters Garden, and check out the gift shop. The museum gift shop offers Oneida and Iroquois arts, jewelry, beadwork, books, clothing, and more.

W892 Co. Rd. EE, De Pere, 800-236-2214
oneida-nsn.gov/our-ways/museum/visit

TIP

The Oneida Nation Museum will be relocating to a new, larger facility in the near future. Be sure to check the address before you drive to the museum. This new facility will allow them to display more of their collections!

INDULGE IN DINNER
AT THE UNION HOTEL AND RESTAURANT

If you're looking for fine dining in a historic setting, look no further than the Union Hotel and Restaurant. The Union is a traditional Wisconsin supper club serving relish trays, bread service, classic cocktails, and unbeatable ambiance. It's the perfect date spot with delicious food. On the menu you can expect to see steak, seafood, and potatoes served three different ways. Meals include a salad and a side.

The Union Hotel is named after the Civil War's northern army. Today the business is over 100 years old, fourth-generation family owned, and the Cream City brick building dates to 1883. Current owner McKim Boyd started tending bar at 13 years old and still works in the restaurant, providing excellent hospitality. McKim has grown their wine menu to over 350 bottles, making it one of the best and most extensive cellars in the region.

200 N. Broadway, De Pere, 920-336-6131
unionhoteldepere.com

TIP

After dinner, get the strawberry schaum torte, a supper club classic. It's a delicious combination of meringue, ice cream, and strawberries.

70

IMMERSE YOURSELF IN CULTURAL DISPLAYS

AT THE MULVA CULTURAL CENTER

The Mulva Cultural Center overlooks the Fox River and aims to provide world-class cultural experiences, showcasing diverse traveling exhibits for visitors and the community of De Pere. The stunning $100 million facility opened to the public in December of 2023. The center was envisioned by James J. and Miriam B. Mulva, whose generosity brought this creative space to life. This center provides opportunities for contemplation and inspiration on the subjects of history, science, world religions, art, and pop culture.

In addition to the traveling exhibits, visitors can view films in the state-of-the-art auditorium, learn in educational classrooms, dine at the upscale bistro, browse the gift shop, or admire indoor and outdoor sculptures throughout the grounds. While admission is charged to view the traveling exhibits, the center will offer atrium displays that will always be free to view, making art and cultural displays accessible for all.

221 S Broadway, De Pere, 920-309-8200
mulvacenter.org

STEP INTO
THE HISTORIC HAZELWOOD HOUSE

Hazelwood Historic House is a beautifully preserved Greek Revival home along the Fox River in the Astor Historic District. It was built in 1837–38 by Morgan L. Martin for his wife, Elizabeth Smith Martin. Morgan was a prominent Green Bay attorney and Indian agent who was later elected to and served in the Wisconsin State Assembly. His daughters Sarah and Deborah were civic leaders in the community and played prominent roles in society.

In 1989, ownership of Hazelwood House was transferred to the Brown County Historical Society. It has since been restored, and the historical society continues to preserve the memories and stories of the family that lived in this historic home. Guided tours are available at Hazelwood Historic House by appointment and can be requested via phone or email at bchsvolunteer@browncountyhistoricalsoc.org. Tours are often led by engaging volunteers passionate about the legacy of Hazelwood House.

1008 S Monroe Ave., 920-437-1840
browncohistoricalsoc.org/visit/hazelwood-historic-house-museum-tours

FOLLOW THE PACKERS HERITAGE TRAIL
AS IT TELLS THEIR STORY

Following the Packers Heritage Trail is a great way to see the city of Green Bay. Visitors can drive, bike, or walk to stops along the trail. The trail features 25 landmarks with each having a bronze commemorative plaque sharing the story and significance of the location relating to Packers heritage. There are three sections of the heritage trail including the City Walk, the Packing Plant Spur, and the Lambeau–Lombardi Spur.

The trail can be self-guided, or visitors can take a trolley tour of the trail that departs from Lambeau Field. Stops include Indian and Acme Packing and Plants; Curly Lambeau's office, birthplace home, and grave site; and Vince Lombardi's home. The trolley tour can be booked online or at Lambeau Field, and the self-guided tour is free with the map available for download on packershofandtours.com.

Various locations, 920-569-7512
packershofandtours.com

GET SWEET TREATS AND GIFTS
AT SEROOGY'S

Seroogy's is the oldest chocolate shop in the area and was founded by Seroogy brothers Joe, Jim, and Sol in 1899 selling fine chocolate candies. Seroogy's now has two locations and continues to sell their homemade, hand-dipped chocolates with high-quality ingredients and excellent customer service. Favorite chocolate treats at Seroogy's include the popular melt-away bars, truffles, sea salt caramels, chocolate-covered Oreos and graham crackers, and holiday decorated chocolates. Seroogy's offers a good selection of sugar-free options as well.

In addition to chocolates, Seroogy's offers coffees, teas, popcorn, nuts, gift boxes, and more. In recent years, Seroogy's has won numerous community-voted awards for having the best gift shop in the area. Seroogy's supports local schools, churches, sports teams, music and dance groups, clubs, and community service organizations by providing fundraising opportunities selling their chocolate bars and fresh-roasted coffees.

144 N Wisconsin St., De Pere, 920-336-1383
seroogys.com

TIP

Try their chocolate-covered potato chips for a sweet-and-salty treat! If potato chips aren't your thing, try the chocolate-covered Oreos or graham crackers. You can choose between white-, milk-, or dark-chocolate-covered goodies.

POKE AROUND

POLKA DAYS

Located just 18 miles outside of Green Bay is the village of Pulaski. Pulaski has a rich Polish heritage that is celebrated every year with a four-day polka festival called Pulaski Polka Days. The festival has been celebrated annually for over 45 years and draws thousands of visitors from around the globe to hear some of the best polka music in the world performed live. The four-day event kicks off with fireworks on Thursday night, and the festival continues until Sunday.

At the event you can expect to find Polish cuisine, tons of live music across three performance areas, dance lessons, an arts and crafts festival downtown, a pancake breakfast, and a huge parade. The event takes place at the Pulaski Community Park, which is also known as the "Polka Days Grounds" every July. Tickets can be purchased upon arrival at the entry gates.

429 E Pulaski St., Pulaski
pulaskipolkadays.com

TIP

While you're in Pulaski, be sure to stop by Smurawa's Country Bakery. The bakery is family owned and makes traditional central and eastern European baked goods like kolaches, kneecaps, and paczki. They are well known for their paczki, offering 17 different flavors, and use a family recipe that's more than 90 years old.

75

SEE CITY STADIUM

City Stadium is on Green Bay's east side, and it was the home of the Green Bay Packers for 32 years, from 1925 to 1956. The field is still used as home to the Green Bay East High School football team and remains one of the last landmarks of early NFL history. The stadium originally had 6,000 seats and was expanded to 25,000 seats to accommodate the growing population of Packers fans.

One of the most notable events that occurred here in relation to Packers history was a game played on Thanksgiving Day 1949 that drew 15,000 fans. This game was scheduled in hopes of raising enough money to help the team complete their season. They were facing $90,000 in losses, and this cold game helped to sustain the team. City Stadium is highlighted on the Packers Heritage Trail.

1500 E Walnut St., 920-448-2090

76

ATTEND AN EVENT
AT THE RIVERSIDE BALLROOM

The historic Riverside Ballroom has hosted famous musicians, tons of wedding receptions, and even some politicians. The original ballroom was built in 1927 as a dance hall and skating rink but burned down in 1935. It was rebuilt and announced as "Wisconsin's Finest Most Modern Ballroom" when it reopened in 1936. The rebuild was made of brick and steel, making it fireproof.

Notably, the Riverside Ballroom was the location of the second-to-last performance of Buddy Holly, Ritchie Valens, and J. P. Richardson (known as the Big Bopper), before all three perished in a tragic plane crash on February 3, 1959. In front of the ballroom, there is a tribute to the three musicians. The facility was also used as the Packers' indoor practice field in 1940 and 1942 when the winter weather wasn't conducive to outdoor practice prior to end-of-season games.

1560 Main St., 920-432-5518
riversideballroom.com

TAKE A RIDE
ON ELVIS'S FAVORITE ROLLER COASTER

Built between 1912 and 1917, the Zippin Pippin is one of the oldest existing wooden roller coasters in the United States. It was originally in Memphis, Tennessee, at East End Park before moving to Libertyland amusement park. After Libertyland closed, the city of Green Bay purchased the Zippin Pippin in 2010. It was then installed at the Bay Beach Amusement Park and opened to the public in May of 2011.

The Zippin Pippin was Elvis Presley's favorite roller coaster, and he would occasionally rent out the entirety of Libertyland to ride the coaster uninterrupted. On August 8, 1977, just eight days before his death, Elvis rented out the park from 1 a.m. to 7 a.m. The Zippin Pippin has hills of 35, 38, 45, 54, and 70 feet. It is 2,500 feet long and goes up to 40 mph. Visitors can experience this coaster May through September.

1313 Bay Beach Rd., 920-448-3365
greenbaywi.gov/488/zippin-pippin

GO TO THE NATIONAL SHRINE OF OUR LADY OF CHAMPION

Just over 16 miles from Green Bay, the first and only approved Marian apparition site in the United States is located in Champion, Wisconsin. Adele Brise, a Belgian immigrant, is believed to have seen the Blessed Lady on Sunday, October 9, 1859. Following the Lady's requests, Adele worked to educate children and gathered women to assist in her teaching mission. A convent, school, and wooden chapel were built by the community in 1861.

On October 8, 1871, the most devastating fire in US history broke out. The Great Peshtigo Fire killed more than 1,200 people and burned 1.2 million acres but left the shrine's grounds untouched. In 2016, the United States Conference of Catholic Bishops designated the grounds as a national shrine. Visitors can view the oratory, chapel, grottos, history center, and the Mother of Mercy Hall. The grounds are open with Mass taking place daily.

4047 Chapel Dr., New Franken, 920-866-2571
championshrine.org

VISIT
THE BROWN COUNTY COURTHOUSE

Completed in 1910, the Brown County Courthouse is centrally located downtown and can be recognized by its bell tower and striking copper dome that stand out in the skyline. The courthouse, designed by architect Charles E. Bell, is on the National Register of Historic Places for its artistic and architectural significance. When the courthouse opened to the public, more than 10,000 of the 25,226 county residents came to see it.

By 1986, the courthouse was still in use but in need of many repairs. A five-phase, $10 million renovation began in 1988. Work was completed to restore the artwork and decor throughout the building in 1993. The rotunda has four murals by Franz Soling: *Justice*, *Agriculture*, *Commerce*, and *Industry*. The terrazzo and marble mosaic floors are original along with the tower bell and Seth Thomas clock in the rotunda. The Brown County Courthouse is free to visit.

100 S Jefferson St., 920-448-4110
browncountywi.gov

80

CHECK OUT CLASSIC CARS
AT THE AUTOMOBILE GALLERY

The Automobile Gallery was envisioned by William "Red" Lewis, an innovative entrepreneur and Green Bay native. The contemporary gallery and event space opened in 2016, in the old Denil Cadillac building, a prestigious dealership that operated from 1958 to 1997. The gallery is driven by the phrase "The automobile is the art," and walking through the gallery feels exactly like that phrase. From polished cement floors to shiny vintage cars, the space is stunning.

Over the years, many cars have been donated to the museum. So many, in fact, that the museum has undergone two expansions to store the collection. There are more than 90 classic automobiles spanning 100 years of automotive history for visitors to view. With rotating special guest vehicles, the collection is ever-changing. As a nonprofit organization, the Automobile Gallery is dedicated to providing the community and visitors enjoyment and enrichment, which they do incredibly well.

400 S Adams St., 920-437-9024
theautomobilegallery.org

TIP

Visit the Automobile Gallery during their Annual Shamrock Craft Beer Invitational and admire classic automobiles while sampling craft beers from more than 20 breweries located throughout Wisconsin and Upper Michigan. There are VIP, general admission, and Designated Driver Guest tickets. You will want to buy your tickets in advance for this popular event!

Wonderland Vintage Market

SHOPPING AND FASHION

81

SEARCH FOR TREASURES
AT WONDERLAND VINTAGE MARKET

If you are a vintage or antique enthusiast, Wonderland Vintage Market is sure to bring a smile to your face. Wandering from booth to booth of vintage vendors in search of the perfect find is thrilling here. With more than 40 vendors, you're sure to walk out with a new treasure. You'll see vintage, retro, antique, repurposed, and unique items throughout the market. The vintage market was envisioned by Shaun Dolan, a former De Pere art teacher, and his wife, Kate. Shaun and Kate opened Wonderland Vintage Market in 2020 and have built a community of vintage lovers and enthusiasts in the area.

While visiting the market, be on the lookout for vintage Packers gear, furniture, records, kitchenware, art, and home goods. If you love DIY, you'll be delighted to find Dixie Bell paint products. The market is open Thursday to Tuesday.

1712 Velp Ave., 920-544-9265
wonderlandvintagemarket.com

SNIFF SOAPS AND CANDLES
AT SMITHMAKER ARTISAN CO.

If you're walking along Broadway in De Pere, you'll see a building with a white facade and seasonal window decorations drawing you in; this is SmithMaker Artisan Co. SmithMaker is a gift shop focused on highlighting Wisconsin and Midwest artisans. Their mission is to "celebrate and support the creativity, skill, and community spirit of our artisans." SmithMaker is proud to offer a place for skilled artisans to sell their work.

SmithMaker started in 2020 at the De Pere location and has since expanded to a second location in Sturgeon Bay. This is a great spot to get gifts for your Midwest-loving friends. Inside the shop you'll find clothing, soaps, candles, stationery, drinkware, wine, accessories, and more. If you can't make it into the shop to browse these local goodies, they offer online shopping with options for pickup in-store or shipping.

116 N Broadway, 920-632-7461
smith-maker.com

BROWSE BOOKS
AT LION'S MOUTH BOOKSTORE

Lion's Mouth Bookstore is a downtown independent bookstore selling new and used books, along with a collection of games, journals, bookmarks, stationery, and toys. Lion's Mouth also has a children's section with fun and diverse titles for kids to explore and enjoy. Inside the shop there are dark wood shelves and furniture pieces with rich color tones, making it a cozy space to browse for your new favorite book.

Whether you walk in with a book in mind or with hopes an intriguing title pops out at you, Lion's Mouth Bookstore staff members are excited to help you find it. The bookstore is involved in the community by working with nonprofits and hosting a variety of community events. From book clubs to author-hosted events, you are sure to find bookish community at Lion's Mouth Bookstore.

211 N Washington St., 920-406-0200
lionsmouthbookstore.com

FIND ALL THINGS HERBAL
AT AURORA'S APOTHECARY

Aurora Adelbush, a practicing herbalist, started Aurora's Apothecary over 15 years ago to provide natural remedies and encourage holistic health in the community. Aurora's Apothecary carries specialty teas, dried herbs, essential oils, crystals, books, and more. The specialty teas, essential-oil blends, balms, and sprays can be shopped based on the ailment they seek to improve. Some common ailments shoppers seek products for include digestion, sleep, immune support, stress, and headache relief. The store also has an extensive selection of crystals that come with little description cards to share their significance.

While browsing the selections, you'll find items that are certified as "Something Special from Wisconsin," a state designation that means at least 50 percent of the product is produced, sourced, or processed in Wisconsin. Today Aurora's Apothecary has expanded to four locations in the region including Green Bay, Appleton, Fish Creek, and Fond du Lac.

133 N Broadway, Ste. A, 920-857-3969
aurorasapothecary.com

85

DELIGHT IN BEAUTIFUL BOUQUETS
AT SCHROEDER'S FLOWERS

Schroeder's Flowers has been family owned and operated for over 100 years. Over the years, the shop has received a variety of awards for florists and floral design. At Schroeder's you'll find plants, bouquets, seasonal decor, and gifts. The shop has an indoor section for gifts and arrangement displays as well as greenhouses for indoor and outdoor plants. Floral arrangements can be ordered custom or there are premade options available for purchase each day.

The kind, welcoming staff at Schroeder's is ready to help you order the perfect arrangement for any occasion. Contemporary and traditional floral arrangements are available for anniversaries, holidays, birthdays, graduations, formals, congratulations, and sympathies. In the summer, the shop has the most beautiful hanging baskets on display outside. The shop is open daily but closed on holidays.

1530 S Webster Ave., 920-436-6363
schroederflowers.com

86

SHOP 'TIL YOU DROP
AT BAY PARK SQUARE

Bay Park Square is a Simon mall that houses more than 90 retailers and eateries. When shopping there, you'll find a variety of general and specialty retailers including Old Navy, Kohl's, Aerie, Sephora, LOFT, and Bath & Body Works. In addition to retailers, the mall has Dave and Buster's, 608 Axe Throwing, Marcus Cinema, and a children's play area on site that cater to families looking for things to do. This is great when half of the family wants to catch a movie while the others want to shop!

When it comes time to eat, there are eateries around the mall and a food court with eight vendors inside. Bay Park Square is also home to the largest Hy-Vee supermarket in Wisconsin. Throughout the mall there is free Wi-Fi, and wheelchairs are complimentary. All entrances of the mall are wheelchair- and stroller-accessible. The mall is open daily.

303 Bay Park Sq., 920-499-2277
simon.com/mall/bay-park-square

GET LOCAL PRODUCE
AT THE FARMERS MARKET

The event of the summer in Green Bay is the Farmers' Market on Broadway that takes place Wednesday nights from 3 to 8 p.m. More than 110 vendors fill the streets offering flower bouquets, fresh produce, prepared foods, coffees, teas, cheeses, meats, preserves, artisan goods, and more. There are food trucks where you can grab dinner, a beer tent serving a variety of beers, usually with some being local, and live music playing. Local bars located around the market have live music as well. The Farmers' Market on Broadway has been in existence for over 20 years, and it's estimated that the market sees 250,000 attendees throughout the season.

163 N Broadway

TIP

Another great market to check out is the Saturday Farmers Market on Washington Street from 7 a.m. to noon. The Saturday Farmers Market started in 1917 and has been operating for over 100 years. Here you'll find fresh produce, plants, preserves, flowers, and more. The Saturday Farmers Market is open May to October. It can be found at South Washington and Doty Streets.

MORE FARMERS MARKETS IN GREEN BAY

Winter Market on Military
725 S Military Ave.
Saturdays 9 a.m. to 1 p.m., November to April

Summer Market on Military
216 S Military Ave.
Thursdays 2 to 7 p.m., June to October

Oneida Farmers Market
N7332 Water Circle Pl., Oneida
Thursdays noon to 6 p.m., June to September

88

GEAR UP
AT PETE'S GARAGE

Pete's Garage is a bicycle and endurance sports shop on Broadway in a building that used to be owned by International Harvester as a repair shop and showroom in 1936. Brothers Tyson and Kurt Schwiesow opened Pete's Garage in 2015, naming it after their grandfather, Pete Lorenzen, who owned a bike repair shop in Chicago in the early 1900s. Cycling has been a passion for the two brothers, and bringing this shop to the Broadway District has allowed them to share their passion with others interested in cycling and endurance sports.

The shop has a variety of bikes, clothing, accessories, footwear, helmets, snowshoes, winter gear, and ski gear. Pete's Garage also offers repairs and parts, along with ski and bike rentals. Rentals bike options include mountain bikes, e-bikes, road bikes, and hybrid bikes. Skis can be rented for a day or a weekend.

142 N Broadway, 920-857-1690
petesgarage.com

TIP

Pete's Garage hosts a Tuesday-night group ride or ski depending on the season to build community around endurance sports. The Tuesday-night ride leaves from the shop and has been a huge hit with three different groups to ride among. The three groups cater to cyclists of different experience levels. Event information can be found on the shop's Facebook page: facebook.com/petesgaragegb.

TASTE TEAS FROM AROUND THE WORLD
AT CULTIVATE TASTE

Cultivate Taste is a specialty shop selling loose-leaf teas, tea accessories, and small vegetarian bites to enjoy with tea. The owner of the salon, Jennifer Nowicki, is a certified tea specialist from the Specialty Tea Institute in New York City. Jennifer has 25 years of experience in the tea industry and brings a wealth of knowledge to visitors in her salon. Open Tuesday to Sunday, Cultivate Taste is located in a bright, modern space within the Railyard Innovation District.

Cultivate Taste hosts tea-tasting events focusing on a shared origin or type of tea for each tasting. Teas at the salon never include flavorings, sugar, or candy to maintain the integrity and quality of the teas. Teas are single-origin and fair-trade wherever possible, and they're sold in eco-friendly biodegradable packaging to reduce impact on the environment.

520 N Broadway, Ste. 120, 920-770-7163
cultivatetaste.com

90

SAMPLE OLIVE OILS
AT OILERIE

Oilerie is an olive oil shop that has been in business since 2003. The inspiration for the shop came from trips to Europe that owners Amy Jo and Curt Campbell had taken where they observed how olive oil was sold there. The store sells spices, Italian snacks and ingredients, and olive oil in Italian-made canisters, offering tastings and bottle fillings. The owners went on *Shark Tank* (episode 604) but left with no deal. They were the first store in the US to offer olive oil in a dispensary format. They also appeared on *After the Tank*, a series to check in on how the business has done since their appearance on *Shark Tank*.

The store sources their olive oils directly from Italy, getting their olive oil from the Montova family in Lazio. The Oilerie has an online store and a physical space in Bellevue. The Oilerie is a foodie's dream shop.

2064 Lime Kiln Rd., Ste. 4, 920-857-2331
oilerie.com

TIP

If you're shopping for a gift, a basket of Italian goodies is always a great idea. Whether you choose a premade gift basket in-store or choose items yourself, you're sure to walk out with the perfect gift.

SHOP WITH PURPOSE
AT SUNRISE ON MAIN BOUTIQUE

Sunrise on Main is an upscale women's boutique in Green Bay's Historic Olde Main District that sells like-new fashionable pieces. Sunrise on Main has shoes, dresses, jackets, coats, tops, skirts, pants, handbags, and accessories displayed in the main room along with a vintage hall and a room for formal wear. The boutique relies on donations of upscale, fashionable, designer, and vintage items, which they do well with. Any items received in donations that don't fit their store's requirements are redonated to other area charities.

Proceeds from each sale at Sunrise on Main go to Reset.Life, a local women's charity. Funds from the boutique help provide life-coaching programs to women who are hoping to reset their life or are in need of support. At Sunrise on Main, you can "shop for yourself and uplift someone else." The boutique is open Tuesday to Saturday.

1244 Main St., 920-857-1662
sunriseonmain.com

FIND GLOBAL FLAVORS
AT INTERNATIONAL FOOD MARKETS

Experience the diversity of cultures in Green Bay through discovering new foods. There are more than 12 international food markets in Green Bay showcasing a variety of foods from Indian, Asian, Somali and other African, Mexican, Italian, and Hispanic cultures. If you're looking for global flavors, ingredients, snacks, and sweets, check out these international markets.

Xiong Oriental Market offers a variety of foods from Asian countries. Specialty grocery items sold include rice, sauces, spices, curry pastes, chilis, soy sauce, soft drinks, teas, candies, snacks, and fresh and frozen produce items, along with cookware, kitchenware, and knives.

Asian Taste Supermarket and Main Oriental Market offer foods and goods primarily from Asian countries. India Bazaar Green Bay and Astha Grocery and Gifts offer items primarily from Indian cuisines. Mexican grocery items can be found at La Espiga, a local tortilleria and supermarket, and at Mi Tierra Food Market. Makélélésho African Shop provides a variety of African food items.

INTERNATIONAL MARKETS

Xiong Oriental Market
610 Bodart St., 920-932-9297

Asian Taste Supermarket
722 Bodart St., 920-431-8439

Main Oriental Market
607 Pine St., 920-435-5271

Astha Grocery and Gifts
582 Redbird Cir., De Pere, 920-632-6435

Mi Tierra Food Market
1333 Cedar St., 920-435-6179

La Espiga
1606 Main St., 920-430-1784

India Bazaar Green Bay
2321 S Oneida St., Ste. 4, 920-425-3018

Makélélésho African Shop
521 E Walnut St., 509-217-5178

PERUSE HANDCRAFTED GOODS
AT TURTLE ISLAND GIFTS

Choose from a diverse collection of art made by local and Native American artists at Turtle Island Gifts. The store was opened by Darleen Denny, an Oneida artist herself, with a mission to bring other artists' work to light and provide a space for artists to sell their work year-round. The work of over 35 artists is featured in the store, including jewelry, pottery, art, beads, clothing, crystals, stones, and more.

The store also sells baskets from the local Oneida Basket Guild, made up of over 40 members. A variety of wood is used to make the baskets from willow, pine needle, cedar bark, and black ash. Turtle Island Gifts also hosts yoga, sound immersions, reiki, and "Meet the Artist" events in collaboration with the Inward Bound Gallery next door.

1641 Commanche Ave., Ste. C, Ashwaubenon, 920-785-4318

GET GREEN BAY SOUVENIRS AT LOCO WISCO

LoCo WisCo is a souvenir shop that sells items from more than 100 small Wisconsin-based businesses and makers. The owners, Dena and Micheal Mooney, are fellow travelers who love souvenirs and are always searching for the best things to bring home from a trip. Passionate about souvenirs and Wisconsin, they've designed the store to feel like a small-town Wisconsin tavern. They even play polka music, which is incredibly popular in Wisconsin due to early European settlers immigrating to the state from Germany, Poland, and other Eastern European countries.

At LoCo WisCo, you'll find a variety to choose from while you're on the hunt for your perfect Green Bay souvenir. Items include clothing, candles, art, postcards, preserves, snacks, spirits, and more. They are always featuring new products as they find them, so this is a great place for visitors and locals alike looking for goodies from Wisconsin.

112 N Washington St., 920-489-8122
locowisco.com

TIP

If you're a postcard collector or like sending them to family and friends, stock up on them here! They have the best selection in the area.

TRY ON NEW FASHIONS
AT HEY, DAISY

When it comes to women's boutiques, Green Bay is fortunate to have a variety of choices. A personal favorite for clothing and gift items is hey, daisy, a prominent women's boutique with two locations and an online store. Opened in 2002, hey, daisy is a family-owned business that has been in operation for over 20 years. They offer trendy, affordable clothing, must-have pieces, and wardrobe staples, aiming to be "where fashion meets real life." In addition to clothing and accessories, hey, daisy offers gift items like candles, shower bombs, jewelry, and more. Shop for your next favorite outfit at hey, daisy!

124 N Broadway, Ste. AA, De Pere, 920-336-3247
4199 Main St., Fish Creek
heydaisy.com

OTHER WOMEN'S FASHION BOUTIQUES

Besselli
This boutique sells brands like Free People, Splendid, and Traffic People along with home goods.
201 N Broadway, 920-884-0202

Twist Boutique
If you are looking for quality clothing made in the USA and unique designs, shop here.
760 Willard Dr., Ste. 414, 920-445-3374
twistboutique.com

A Bag Lady
This place is full of fun and bright accessories.
127 N Broadway, 920-430-1839

ZuLou
If you love trend-forward, comfortable clothing, this is your place.
128 N Broadway, 920-857-1251

AZURE
Curated, contemporary clothing is their mainstay.
113 N Wisconsin St., De Pere, 920-347-2720
azurewi.com

Studio Reverie
Their fashion has a minimalist, modern style.
105 S Broadway, De Pere, 920-425-3480
studioreverieclothing.com

LOCATE LUXURY SKIN-CARE PRODUCTS AT VERDE

Verde is the largest full-service clean skin-care market north of Chicago. Products in the store are researched, vetted, and handpicked by owner Lori Buss-Michaelis. Lori has 22 years of experience in the skin-care industry and is passionate about making clean beauty accessible to the area by providing options of clean products that fit a variety of skin-care needs and budgets. Verde Market also has aestheticians providing facials, laser treatments, and injections. The space feels welcoming and is beautifully decorated.

At Verde you'll find luxury clean makeup, clean beauty options, supplements, gift sets, and some travel products as well. The clean beauty and skin-care products in the market are chemical-free and contain no sulfates or parabens. The market also has a "dirty corner" that contains items that might not be considered clean products, but they are unique items that aren't available anywhere else in the area.

115 N Broadway, De Pere, 920-247-9367
shopverdemarket.com

97

GAZE UPON FINE JEWELRY

AT BAY AREA DIAMOND COMPANY

Bay Area Diamond Company has been serving the Green Bay community for over 18 years, and over that time they have expanded to two other locations in the Midwest. Bay Area Diamond Company offers high-quality jewelry and customer service. If you're shopping for jewelry, you'll want to check out their selection. They have watches, earrings, pendants, wedding bands, engagement rings, and fashion rings. In addition to their showroom selection, they offer jewelry repair, appraisals, laser engraving, and even custom jewelry design. To keep your pieces protected, they offer a lifetime warranty.

One of the things that makes Bay Area Diamond Company so unique is where they source their diamonds. Owners Brian and Jill Rouse travel to Antwerp, Belgium, the diamond capital of the world, each year to purchase diamonds for the store and for customers' custom jewelry designs. Diamonds they purchase are conflict-free, handcrafted, and carefully selected.

225 S Military Ave., 920-494-0002
bayareadiamond.com

98

SHOP
AT MAPLEWOOD MEATS

Maplewood Meats started in 1983 as a 10-foot meat case and local processing facility. Over 40 years later, they are now serving the entire state of Wisconsin in addition to providing services throughout the United States. In early 2024, an expansion and remodel were announced by Maplewood Meats. The expansion will feature a shopping area and to-go vending to better serve their customers.

Maplewood Meats' mission is to "craft products using old-fashioned techniques and unique natural smoking processes." Their quality cuts and delicious smoked meats have made them a favorite among locals and has gained them a loyal customer base. At Maplewood Meats, you'll find sausages, snack sticks, brats, steaks, beef tenderloin, hickory-smoked ham, smoked bacon, and so much more. You can shop and browse the selections in-store, order for pickup, or order online for delivery options.

4663 Milltown Rd., 920-865-7901
maplewoodmeats.com

TIP

While you're picking up snack sticks and fresh meat cuts at Maplewood Meats, be sure to grab some cheese from Renard's in the market as well. Renard's Cheese is a cheese-making business based in Sturgeon Bay. I highly recommend pairing Maplewood Meats snack sticks and Renard's string cheese for a road-trip snack!

GET SQUEAKY CHEESE CURDS

FROM SCRAY CHEESE

Established in 1924, Scray Cheese Co. is a fourth-generation artisan cheese factory based in De Pere, specializing in making delicious gouda, fontina, and cheddar. The Scray Cheese Shoppe sells more than 100 types of cheeses from Wisconsin. If you're looking for fresh squeaky cheese curds, look no further than Scray Cheese.

If you're eating truly fresh cheese curds, they should squeak against your teeth as you chew. This is either something that will bring you immense joy and childlike wonder or you might absolutely hate it. Scray Cheese has classic cheddar cheese curds and a variety of seasoned cheese curds to enjoy.

Another reason to visit Scray Cheese is their cheese-making viewing window that allows you to see fresh cheese curds being made. Cheese is made Monday through Thursday and on Saturday. The best time to see cheese-making in action is on weekday mornings.

2082 Old Martin Rd., De Pere, 920-347-0303
scraycheese.com

TIP

The freshest cheese curds, which are the squeakiest, are available Monday, Tuesday, Thursday, and Saturday! Cheese curds are squeaky for up to three days after they are made.

BUY SOURDOUGH BREAD
AT VOYAGEURS BAKEHOUSE

Founded by Ben Cadman and Celeste Parins in 2018, Voyageurs Bakehouse is the best place to get fresh sourdough bread in Green Bay. Located in the Rail Yard Innovation District on Broadway, their unique open-concept, modern bakehouse is simply stunning. In the bakehouse, you can pick from a variety of sourdough loaves and baked goods, or enjoy an item from their café menu. Watching bread-making through the panes of glass in the bakehouse is a delightful sight. Freshly baked bread is available in the bakehouse Tuesday to Saturday.

One thing that makes Voyageurs Bakehouse bread locally significant is their use of Wisconsin-grown grains. Voyageurs Bakehouse partners with a variety of local businesses sourcing ingredients, from grains to eggs, to make their delicious artisan products. If you're into farm-to-table, stopping by Voyageurs Bakehouse should certainly be on your bucket list.

340 N Broadway, Ste. 110, 920-234-8060
voyageurs.co

TIP

Stop at Voyageurs Bakehouse for a coffee break. Order a coffee from the barista and an espresso rye chocolate chip cookie for some sweetness with a bit of added caffeine. The coffee and espresso used in the bakehouse are from Coffee Wizardz, a fantastic local coffee shop.

ACTIVITIES
BY SEASON

SPRING

SUMMER

FALL

WINTER

SUGGESTED ITINERARIES

GAME DAY WEEKEND

FAMILY FUN DAYS

FOODIES' DELIGHT

HISTORY BUFFS

Al's Hamburgers

INDEX

Packers Hall of Fame